New Frontiers In Second Language Learning

Edited by

JOHN H. SCHUMANN
Harvard University

NANCY STENSON
University of California
San Diego

NEWBURY HOUSE PUBLISHERS, INC.

NEWBURY HOUSE PUBLISHERS, Inc.

Language Science
Language Teaching
Language Learning

68 Middle Road, Rowley, Massachusetts 01969

ISBN: 912066-84-9 (paper)
         912066-54-7 (cloth)

First Printing: February, 1975

Printed in the U.S.A.   Second Printing: June, 1976

LIST OF CONTRIBUTORS

RONALD WARDHAUGH
University of Michigan

MAGDELHAYNE F. BUTEAU
McGill University

JACK C. RICHARDS
Regional English Language Center, Singapore

NANCY STENSON
University of California, San Diego

MARINA K. BURT
State University of New York, Albany

CAROL KIPARSKY
Teacher of English as a Second Language

FREDA HOLLEY
University of Texas, Austin

JANET K. KING
University of Texas, Austin

S. P. CORDER
University of Edinburgh

LARRY SELINKER
University of Washington

JOHN H. SCHUMANN
Harvard University

ROAR RAVEM
University College for Teachers, Norway

ACKNOWLEDGEMENTS

The editors wish to thank the authors who agreed to allow us to reprint or publish for the first time the articles appearing in this book. We also thank the publishers of the various journals for granting us permission to reprint the articles.

We would also like to thank Bruce Fraser, Associate Professor, Psycholinguistics Program, Boston University, who provided us with initial encouragement as well as many helpful suggestions while compiling this collection of readings. Finally we wish to express our thanks to Francine M. Schumann for her help in designing the cover for *New Frontiers in Second Language Learning*.

TABLE OF CONTENTS

a.
INTRODUCTION

JOHN H. SCHUMANN & NANCY STENSON

Research in foreign language teaching has recently begun to direct itself toward an increased understanding of second language acquisition. As with any research, new theoretical and methodological concepts emerge as old ones are proved inadequate. Among the concepts which have been discussed in the TESOL literature over the past several years, we have seen first linguistic analysis, then contrastive analysis, and most recently error analysis. What is most often called error analysis is largely a non-American tradition; it has aroused much interest throughout the rest of the English-speaking world, but for the most part, American scholars have continued to advocate contrastive analysis as the ultimate panacea for language teaching problems and have tended to ignore the potential contributions of more recent research. In view of the controversy surrounding these disciplines, a certain amount of background is needed to place them in perspective.

Linguistic analysis, most simply stated, is the work done by linguists in providing a descriptive grammar of a language. Linguistic analysis was initially done within the prescriptive framework of Latin grammar, later during the first half of the 20th century, within the structuralist framework, and most recently within the framework of generative grammar.

Linguistic analysis is concerned with the competence for his own language which a native speaker possesses, a competence quite different from that which a non-native learner of the language would have. For this reason, generative linguists have expressed doubt as to the value of linguistic analysis to the language teacher. The following statement of the issue was made by Chomsky at the 1966 Northeast Conference:

> I am frankly skeptical about the significance, for the teaching of language of such insights and understanding as have been attained in linguistics and psychology. It is possible—even likely—that principles of psychology and linguistics, and research in these disciplines, may supply insights useful to the language teacher. But this must be demonstrated, and cannot be presumed. It is the language teacher himself who must validate or refute any specific proposal.

Certainly the grammar of a transformational linguist would not be useable as a teaching grammar, being far too abstract and formal to adapt to classroom use. However, the insights gained by linguistic analysis have more than once been used by pedagogues in developing materials for language teaching. Most notably the Audio-Lingual Method, still widely used in U.S. schools, was based on the tenets underlying structural linguistics, and both its merits and its defects have been found to follow from those which further study has revealed in the parent theory. Many of the more recent insights gained by research in transformational generative grammar may likewise be useful to the language teacher, if not in providing actual teaching material, then at least in providing a better understanding of certain student problems. As research continues, insights into the learning process will hopefully enable teachers to better understand some of what goes on in the classroom from a psycholinguistic point of view. So far, however, the linguistic research currently being carried on is far too tentative to be of much use in teaching.

The goals of contrastive analysis are more specifically pedagogical. Wardhaugh's article in this volume points out that contrastive analysis exists in both a strong and a weak form. The strong version embodies a claim of predictive power: that a contrastive analysis of two languages can be used to predict the errors that speakers of the first language will make in learning the second, and thus can be used directly in the development of teaching materials. As Wardhaugh points out, this position is untenable at present, for it makes demands that cannot be met on linguistic theory and a non-existent theory of contrastive analysis. It is, however, the version that underlies much of the work that has been done in contrastive analysis.

The weak version approaches the problem from the opposite direction, taking the purpose of contrastive analysis to be the account of *observed* errors by starting with classroom data and using the differences between the two linguistic systems to explain the errors. Many contrastive analysis attempts which fail in their claim to meet the demands of the strong formulation do meet at least some of the demands of this latter version—their failure is in not doing *all* they promise.

No theory of contrastive analysis, strong or weak, should be expected to account for all errors of language learning. Much evidence is already available which suggests that many errors are due to target-language rule deviance as well. In addition, there are many errors induced by the classroom situation, but which cannot be considered to be a function of performance (i.e., due to inattention, memory lapse, outside interference, etc.). There is some hope, however, that as linguists sharpen their ability to distinguish between the universals and the idiosyncrasies in a language, at least the weak version of contrastive analysis can become a more useful tool in language learning research.

Arising from the failure of contrastive analysis to adequately account for student errors, references began appearing in the literature to a new technique: error analysis. It has been proposed in several places as an alternative or supplement to contrastive analysis, without its being clearly formulated just what is meant by the term or what its proponents feel are its goals. In fact, error analysis covers a wide range of viewpoints as to its goals and its value to the language teaching field, as is evident from the papers in this volume. It is this vagueness and variety, we feel, that has engendered much of the hostility on the part of the proponents of contrastive analysis.

Error analysis grew out of transformational linguistic theory and the notion of language as a rule-governed system. A serious and oft-noted problem of most contrastive analyses is that they typically concentrate on superficial differences between languages; more recent developments in linguistic research, on the other hand, have indicated that surface forms reveal little about the nature of language, and that more valid insights into language structure are to be found on a more abstract level, a level at which the differences and similarities discovered by contrastive analysis might prove to be irrelevant, or nonexistent. Within such a framework, the error is perceived as a rule violation with respect to the target language alone. Understanding of student learning strategies must depart from this point.

It is apparent when one thinks about what is involved in actually doing an analysis of errors, that there is relatively small difference between it and the weak form of contrastive analysis. The contrastive/error analysis controversy had its origin in the directionality of the analysis: whether one started from the analysis of the language being studied or from the student's performance. This conflict only exists where we take contrastive analysis to mean the strong version, which claims predictive power based on description of the two languages involved.

If we compare the weak form of contrastive analysis to error analysis, we find that in fact they both make their departure from the same point: the target language *as the student speaks it.* Both attempt to account for observed facts. Differences arise at the next step—how to account for the data observed. Contrastive analysis looks for points of interference from the student's native language, while what has been called error analysis considers errors only in terms of the student's formulation of the target language system. These two approaches are not inconsistent, but, rather, focus on different problems within the same approach. We therefore suggest that contrastive analysis in its weak form should be considered just one aspect of the larger area of error analysis. Moreover, both are specific forms of linguistic analysis.

In oversimplified terms, then, we can divide student errors into at least the following three types: errors due to incomplete acquisition of the target grammar (which may in turn be due to either inter- or intra-lingual difficulties), errors due to the exigencies of the teaching/learning situation, and errors due to normal problems of language performance. Many subcategorizations of error types will be seen in the articles which follow. The task of error analysis from this perspective is to explain why one aspect of the target grammar has not been adequately acquired while a second is learned without difficulty. To the extent that this can be done by reliance on the linguistic systems of the two languages, this work is what we characteristically call contrastive analysis. On the other hand, there is evidence that areas of contrast between two languages are not always the areas of greatest difficulty for the learner. It remains for other branches of error analysis to explore these areas of difficulty. The crucial first step in every case is to find the source of the errors made by students. This is the overall task of error analysis, within which all more detailed analyses fall.

The first article in Part I of this volume is Wardhaugh's attack on the "contrastive analysis hypothesis," referred to above. The American language teaching profession throughout the sixties remained devoted to the idea that a linguistic comparison of two language structures could predict areas of difficulty that would be encountered by a language learner. As a result all error was believed to be contrastively based, i.e., assumed to stem from interference between the structures of the source and target languages. Wardhaugh's article represents one of the first major challenges to this belief.

Buteau's article presents evidence from research conducted in Canada that interference is not sufficient to account for difficulties in second language learning. She demonstrates that French sentences which correspond structurally to their English equivalents are not necessarily the easiest to learn by English speakers, that the probability of errors cannot be assessed solely by examining the degree of divergence between the two linguistic structures, and consequently other factors of difficulty must be considered, such as improper generalizations, number of alternatives involved in the choice of a particular structure, and awareness of target language contextual cues.

Richards, in "Error Analysis and Second Language Strategies," extends the range of error analysis with a taxonomy of errors, based on Selinker (in this volume), identifying the following sources of error:

1) Interference: error resulting from the transfer of grammatical and/or stylistic elements from the source language to the target language;

2) Overgeneralization: error caused by extension of target language rules to areas where they do not apply;

3) Performance errors: unsystematic errors that occur as the result of such things as memory lapses, fatigue, confusion, or strong emotion;

4) Markers of transitional competence: error that results from a natural and perhaps inevitable developmental sequence in the second language learning process (by analogy with first language acquisition);

5) Strategies of communication and assimilation: error resulting from the attempt to communicate in the target language without having completely acquired the grammatical forms necessary to do so;

6) Teacher-induced error: error resulting from pedagogical procedures contained in the text or employed by the teacher.

This last type of error is treated in the article by Stenson. "Induced Errors" presents an extensive discussion of transfer of training errors which come about as the result of course design or teaching techniques. Without advocating attempts to eliminate all error, she maintains that certain grammatical insights would help the teacher structure lessons so that whatever being taught is presented with the maximum generalization. Indeed, induced errors have a certain value. Because they result from teaching techniques which force the student to use new or unfamiliar items, they provide information about gaps in student knowledge that would probably not be evident from his spontaneous speech. Distinguishing between teacher-induced error and error which reflects a student's developing competence is important for all those interested in second language acquisition. Given sufficient exposure to the target language, developmental error is likely to disappear naturally and therefore the teacher might decide not to correct it. On the other hand, some induced errors might fossilize and become difficult to eliminate later and therefore would require immediate correction. In either case, a researcher would not want to mistake errors that are merely products of the teaching situation for features of student speech that reflect developmental patterns.

Stenson also stresses the importance and difficulty of knowing what the student meant to say. Intended meaning is equally important for the teacher and psycholinguistic researcher. Often this meaning may be difficult to get at and therefore presents a challenge to both. A mutual goal might be the development of techniques which provide access to the student's intended meaning.

From Buteau, Richards, and Stenson, we get a detailed analysis of the multiple sources of student error. In the next paper, Burt and Kiparsky offer a practical procedure for error correction. They organize and discuss certain error types from the point of view of the language being studied, in this case English, and then set up a hierarchy of errors based on sentence comprehensibility. In general terms, the authors discover that errors within a constituent or a clause affect the comprehension of a sentence far less than errors which are made in major constituent order or across clause boundaries. In other words, errors in pluralization, article usage, tense usage, etc. are less important in terms of sentence comprehensibility than are errors in word order, or the choice and placement of appropriate connectors. Since no teacher has time to adequately deal with all the errors made by his students, the hierarchy developed by Burt and Kiparsky serves as a guide to those errors on which most time should be spent in order to give the student the greatest possible mileage in terms of acquiring the ability to communicate in the second language.

Holley and King, in the sixth article, take the position that foreign language students should be allowed and perhaps even encouraged to produce ungrammatical sentences. They base their hypothesis on studies of first language acquisition which indicate that mothers tend to correct only those utterances made by their children which are factually inaccurate; mothers do not correct their children's grammatical errors. What a child seems to do is to form a series of increasingly complete hypotheses about the structure of the language he is learning. Within this framework, ungrammatical utterances are not regarded as errors, but rather as evidence of hypothesis formation and language development. The authors feel that these findings offer the foreign language teacher a new point of view from which current classroom techniques for dealing with error can be reevaluated and improved. They present a classroom approach for the teaching of German that incorporates these ideas. Teachers are given specific procedures and guidelines for dealing with student errors. Holley and King describe an experiment in which techniques based on the above assumptions seemed to produce greater participation and interaction between students and instructors. Their conclusion is a suitable theme for this whole volume: "Student errors should be dealt with as a necessary feature of experimentation in the language."

The second part of the volume is more theoretical and deals with the potential contribution that error analysis holds for increasing our understanding of second language acquisition.

In recent years a school of thought has developed which regards the speech of a second language learner at any point in the acquisition process as a systematic attempt to deal with the target language data. That is to say, the utterances of such a learner are not mistakes or deviant forms, but rather are part of a separate but nevertheless genuine linguistic system.

Corder, in "The Significance of Learners' Errors," proposes that the process of language acquisition is essentially the same for both first and second language learning. He believes that while the biological predisposition to acquire one's native language may be replaced by some other force in the learning of a second language, the basic capacity for language acquisition and the strategies employed in both processes are fundamentally the same.

Within this framework a second language learner's errors are similar to those of a child acquiring his first language. They are both systematic and as such give evidence of the system to which they belong. Corder distinguishes between errors and mistakes. The latter are the random slips of the tongue, or performance failures made by all speakers. They are not systematic and are of no significance in language learning. Errors inform the teacher how far along the student is in the learning process; they provide the researcher with evidence of how a second language is acquired, and they provide the learner with a way of forming and testing hypotheses about the nature of the language he is learning.

In "Idiosyncratic Dialects and Error Analysis," a further development of his theory, Corder defines the spontaneous speech of a second language learner as a language having a genuine grammar of its own. He calls this learner language an idiosyncratic dialect, which he distinguishes from both a social dialect and an idiolect. Idiosyncratic dialects are usually unstable and tend to evolve during the language learning process.

In a third article, "Describing the language learner's language,"[1] Corder distinguishes between what might be called remedial and developmental error analysis. The former is used by the teacher as a technique for evaluating and correcting students' classroom errors. The latter is used by the researcher to describe the successive "états de dialecte" of the language learner. The relevant data in an investigation of "état de dialecte" are all utterances, whether grammatical or not, in the target language. Thus the learner is never speaking the target dialect, but a dialect of his own which may share many features of the target language. "The whole corpus of the infant's or the learner's output is relevant to the description of his language systems at any point in his learning career. The well-formedness or appropriateness of his utterances in terms of the adult language is irrelevant." (p. 61).

For Corder, the concept of ungrammaticality does not apply to the second language learner. All utterances in the learner's idiosyncratic dialect (exclusive of performance errors) are acceptable. Longitudinal studies of the successive stages in development of this learner language are necessary in order to begin to understand the process of second language acquisition.

Nemser, in a related article which is not included here but which the reader might wish to consult,[2] identifies the learner language as an "approximative system" which is defined as a structurally cohesive linguistic system distinct from both the source language and the target language. It is by definition transient and is gradually restructured in successive stages from initial through advanced learning. According to Nemser, the ultimate goal of the study of such systems would be the accurate projection of the approximative system throughout its successive stages of development in each contact situation.

Selinker, in "Interlanguage," suggests that there is a *latent psychological structure* in the brain which is activated when one attempts to learn a second language, i.e., whenever one tries to produce a set of sentences in the second language using meanings one may already have. When such an attempt is made, the utterances which are realized are identical neither to those which would have been produced by a native speaker of the target language, nor to the sentences having the same meaning in the learner's native language. Thus a separate linguistic system is hypothesized to account for the actual realized utterances. This system is called "interlanguage."

Selinker identifies five processes as central to second language learning: (1) language transfer, (2) transfer of training, (3) learning strategies, (4) communication strategies, (5) over-generalization. According to Selinker, these five processes force fossilizable material upon the surface structures of the learner's interlanguage. Fossilizations are forms, phonological, morphological, and syntactic, in the speech of a speaker of a second language that do not conform to the target language norms even after years of instruction in and exposure to the standard forms. They also include those forms which, though absent from a learner's speech under normal conditions, tend to reappear in his linguistic performance when he is forced to deal with very difficult material, when he is in a state of anxiety, or when he is extremely relaxed. This systematic backsliding of certain linguistic forms toward the interlingual norms leads Selinker to hypothesize the psychological reality of fossilizations and interlanguages. The goal of a theory of second language learning, according to Selinker, then, would be to describe the knowledge underlying interlingual behavior and to predict the surface structures of the utterances produced in the interlanguage.

The article by Schumann views the processes of pidginization and creolization as models for adult second language acquisition. In analyzing the function of language into three components: communication, affirmation of social identity, and expression of psychological need, pidgins are seen as being functionally restricted to the first component—communication. As a result, pidginization produces interlanguage which is simplified and reduced. When the function of the language of a second language learner is also restricted to communication (as is the usual case in the initial stages of learning), we can expect a learner's interlanguage to reflect some of the simplifications and reductions that are found in pidgins. In the process of creolization, the function of language extends to the integrative and expressive uses mentioned above. Concomitant with this extension in function is the complication and expansion of the language structure. In a parallel fashion, when a second language learner attempts to mark his social identity within the target culture or to use his pidginized interlanguage for expressive purposes, we can expect his interlanguage to complicate and expand in ways similar to those fostered by creolization. Thus, the study of pidginization and creolization can provide valuable insights into the second language learning process.

The final article, "The Development of Wh-Questions in First and Second Language Learners," is an example of the type of longitudinal study recommended by Corder. It presents findings concerning the development of Wh-questions (*what, when, where, why, who,* and *how*) in two Norwegian children acquiring English as a second Language and relates them to similar studies of first language acquisition by Roger Brown and his associates. The author's conclusion is that the similarities between both processes are striking, but not necessarily what one would expect. This paper represents a prototype of the kind of research that should be undertaken in the second language acquisition of both children and adults. Longitudinal studies such as this one can eventually provide us with concrete data on the second language learning process.

As was mentioned earlier, error analysis has not aroused widespread interest as yet in the United States. It is interesting to note that British and Canadian linguists were never so taken with the contrastive analysis hypothesis as were the Americans, and continued to recognize multiple sources of student error. Thus, error analysis is new to American language teaching circles, and it is hoped that this volume will bring its insights to bear on the theoretical and practical aspects of language learning and teaching in the U.S.

FOOTNOTES

[1]Corder, S.P. "Describing the language learner's language," *Interdisciplinary Approaches to Language. CILT Reports and Papers 6.* September 1971, pp. 57-64 (not included in this book).

[2]Nemser, W. "Approximative Systems of Foreign Language Learners," *International Review of Applied Linguistics.* Vol. IX, No. 2, 1971, pp. 115-123.

b.

THE CONTRASTIVE ANALYSIS HYPOTHESIS

RONALD WARDHAUGH

1.0 *Introduction*

Students of linguistics encounter a number of very interesting hypotheses concerning different aspects of language and language function. One long-lived hypothesis which has attracted considerable attention from time to time—but more, it must be added, from psychologists and anthropologists than from linguists—is the Sapir-Whorf hypothesis with its claim that the structure of a language subtly influences the cognitive processes of the speakers of that language.

A much more recent hypothesis, and one much more intriguing to linguists today than the Sapir-Whorf hypothesis, is the language-acquisition-device hypothesis proposed by the generative-transformationalists. This hypothesis is that infants are innately endowed with the ability to acquire a natural language and all they need to set the process of language acquisition going are natural language data. Only by postulating such a language-acquisition-device can a generative-transformationalist account for certain linguistic universals, including, of course, not only one very important universal, the ability to learn a first language with ease, but also, apparently, another universal, the inability to learn a second language after childhood without difficulty. Like the Sapir-Whorf hypothesis, the language-acquisition-device hypothesis is extremely intriguing, but it too presents seemingly insurmountable difficulties to anyone seeking to devise a critical test of its truth or falsity. A linguist may accept the hypothesis because they usefully and economically explain certain language data that he seeks to account for according to a set of axioms he can accept; or he may reject the hypotheses because they appear to be mentalistic or subjective, or because he prefers a different set of axioms for his work.

Still a third hypothesis is the contrastive-analysis hypothesis, a hypothesis of particular interest to those linguists who are engaged in language teaching and in writing language-teaching materials. However, the contrastive-analysis hypothesis also raises many difficulties in practice, so many in fact that it is tempting to ask whether it is really possible to make contrastive analyses. And, even if the answer to that question is a more or less hesitant affirmative, then one may well question the value to teachers and curriculum workers of the results of such analyses.

2.0 *The Strong Version*

The contrastive analysis hypothesis may be stated in two versions, a *strong version* and a *weak version*. The strong version seems quite unrealistic and impracticable, even though it is the one on which those who write contrastive analyses usually claim to base their work. On the other hand, the weak version does have certain possibilities for usefulness. However, even the weak version is suspect in some linguistic circles.

It is possible to quote several representative statements of the strong version of the contrastive-analysis hypothesis. First of all, Lado in the preface to *Linguistics Across Cultures* (1957) writes as follows:

> The plan of the book rests on the assumption that we can predict and describe the patterns that will cause difficulty in learning, and those that will not cause difficulty, by comparing systematically the language and culture to be learned with the native language and culture of the student. (p. vii)

Since Lado cites Fries in support of this proposition, an appropriate quotation from Fries's *Teaching and Learning English as a Foreign Language* (1945) would be the following one:

> The most efficient materials are those that are based upon a scientific description of the language to be learned, carefully compared with a parallel description of the native language of the learner. (p. 9)

More recently, in Valdman's *Trends in Language Teaching* (1966), Banathy, Trager, and Waddle (1966) state the strong version of the contrastive-analysis hypothesis as follows:

> . . .the change that has to take place in the language behavior of a foreign language student can be equated with the differences between the structure of the student's native language and culture and that of the target language and culture. The task of the linguist, the cultural anthropologist, and the sociologist is to identify these differences. The task of the writer of a foreign language teaching program is to develop materials which will be based on a statement of these differences; the task of the foreign language teacher is to be aware of these differences and to be prepared to teach them; the task of the student is to learn them. (p. 37)

The same idea is presented in each of these three statements, the idea that it is possible to contrast the system of one language—the grammar, phonology, and lexicon—with the system of a second language in order to *predict* those difficulties which a speaker of the second language will have in learning the first language and to construct teaching materials to help him learn that language.

An evaluation of this strong version of the contrastive-analysis hypothesis suggests that it makes demands of linguistic theory, and, therefore, of linguists, that they are in no position to meet. At the very least this version demands of linguists that they have available a set of linguistic universals formulated within a comprehensive linguistic theory which deals adequately with syntax, semantics, and phonology. Furthermore, it requires that they have a theory of contrastive linguistics into which they can plug complete linguistic descriptions of the two languages being contrasted so as to produce the correct set of contrasts between the two languages. Ideally, linguists should not have to refer at all to speakers of the two languages under contrast for either confirmation or disconfirmation of the set of contrasts generated by any such theory of contrastive linguistics. They should actually be able to carry out their contrastive studies quite far removed from speakers of the two languages, possibly without even knowing anything about the two languages in question except what is recorded in the grammars being used. Such seems to be the procedure which the strong version of the contrastive-analysis hypothesis demands of linguists. Stated in this way, the strong version doubtless sounds quite unrealistic, but it should be emphasized that *most writers of contrastive analyses try to create the impression that this is the version of the hypothesis on which they have based their work*—or at least *could* base their work if absolutely necessary. Here is yet another instance of a "pseudo-procedure" in linguistics, a pseudo-procedure being a procedure which linguists claim they could follow in order to achieve definitive results if only there were enough time.

Any examination of how phonological problems have been dealt with in this strong version easily produces evidence to support the assertions just made. Many a linguist has presented contrastive statements of the phonemic systems of two languages without asking whether it is possible to contrast the phonemic systems of two languages by procedures which attempt to relate an English p to a French p, because linguists have chosen to symbolize some not well-defined similarity between the two languages in the same way, in this case by the letter p, or because both p's are associated with certain movements of the glottis and lips. The use of the similarity of the symbols is more deceiving than the use of the similarity of phonetic features. The latter may be justified to some extent in terms of what will be referred to later as the weak version of the hypothesis, but statements about a language *lacking* certain phonemes or two languages having the *same* phonemes are possibly even more dangerous than they are naive. Any such statements must ultimately rest on phonetic evidence, and, if they do, the strong version of the hypothesis is being disregarded in favor of the weak version. As Weinreich (1953) points out, phonemes are not commensurable across languages; phones, the individual sounds, are much more manageable, because they do have some connection with events in the world, in this case articulatory and acoustic events.

Let us suppose that a linguist contrasts the allophonic variants described in accounts he finds of the phonological system of two languages. Could he then meet the demands of the strong version? Once again the answer must be negative, at least within the present state of linguistic knowledge. Ideally, a linguist interested in making a contrastive analysis would like to be able to take a statement of the allophones of Language A and say for each one exactly what difficulties a speaker of Language B would have in producing that allophone. However, the difficulties in the way of doing this are formidable. Are the phonetic statements the linguist finds sufficiently detailed and of the right kind to be of use: that is, what is the adequacy of the *phonetic theory* and of the particular phonetic information at his disposal? Do the descriptions take into account all the phonological variables that should be taken into account, such as segmentation, stress, tone, pitch, and juncture, and syllable, morpheme, word and sentence structures: that is, what is the state of the *phonological theory* he is using? Does the linguist have available to him an over-all contrastive system within which he can relate the two languages in terms of mergers, splits, zeroes, over-differentiations, under-differentiations, reinterpretations, and so on: that is, what is the state of the *contrastive theory* he is employing? In this age of linguistic uncertainty the answer to all of these questions is obvious.

3.0 *The Weak Version*

The weak version requires of the linguist only that he use the best linguistic knowledge available to him in order to account for observed difficulties in second-language learning. It does not require what the strong version requires, the prediction of those difficulties and, conversely, of those learning points which do not create any difficulties at all. The weak version leads to an approach which makes fewer demands of contrastive theory than does the strong version. It starts with the evidence provided by linguistic interference and uses such evidence to explain the similarities and differences between systems. There should be no mistake about the emphasis on systems. In this version systems *are* important, because there is no regression to any pre-systemic view of language, nor does the approach result in merely classifying errors in any way that occurs to the investigator. However, the starting point in the contrast is provided by actual evidence from such phenomena as faulty translation, learning difficulties, residual foreign accents, and so on, and reference is made to the two systems only in order to explain actually observed interference phenomena.

A close reading of most of the contrastive analyses which are available shows them to conform to some of the demands made by the weak version of the theory and not at all to the demands of the strong version. Even the two highly regarded texts on English and Spanish by Stockwell and Bowen, *The Sounds of English and Spanish* (1965) and *The Grammatical Structures of English and Spanish* (1965), fall into this category. It appears that Stockwell and Bowen use their linguistic knowledge to explain what they know from experience to be problems English speakers have in learning Spanish. The linguistic theory they use is actually extremely eclectic and contains insights from generative-transformational, structural, and paradigmatic grammars; nowhere in the texts is there an obvious attempt to predict errors using an over-riding contrastive theory of any power. Even the hierarchy of difficulty which Stockwell and Bowen establish in the second chapter of the *Sounds* volume is based more on their experience and intuition than on an explicit theory for predicting difficulties.

4.0 *Some Recent Claims*

In recent years two still different approaches have been taken to the problems of contrastive analysis, both resulting from the current enthusiasm for generative-transformational theory. One of these approaches dismisses the hypothesis from any consideration at all. This dismissal stems from a strong negative reaction to contrastive analysis, as, for example, in articles by Ritchie (1967) and Wolfe (1967) in *Language Learning*. The second approach attempts to use generative-transformational theory to provide some of the necessary over-riding theory to meet either the demands of prediction in the strong version or of explanation in the weak version.

The case for dismissal may be stated as follows: Languages do not differ from each other without limit in unpredictable ways, statements to the contrary notwithstanding. All natural languages have a great deal in common so that anyone who has learned one language already *knows* a great deal about any other language he must learn. Not only does he know a great deal about that other language even before he begins to learn it, but the deep structures of both languages are very much alike, so that the actual differences between the two languages are really quite superficial. However, to learn the second language, one must learn the precise way in which that second language relates the deep structures to its surface structures and their phonetic representations. Since this way is unique for each language, contrastive analysis can be of little or no help at all in the learning task because the rules to be internalized are unique. Even though the form and some of the content of the rules to be acquired might be identical for both languages, the combinations of these for individual languages are quite idiosyncratic so that superficial contrastive statements can in no way help the learner in his task.

There is obviously some merit in the above argument. If the underlying vowel system of French is something like the one Schane outlines in *French Phonology and Morphology* (1968), and the underlying vowel system of English is something like the one Chomsky and Halle outline in *The Sound Pattern of English* (1968), and if the speaker of English must somehow internalize the underlying vowel system of French and the fifty or so phonetic realization rules which Schane gives in order to speak acceptable French, then one may easily be tempted to reject the whole notion of contrastive analysis, claiming that it has nothing at all to contribute to an understanding of the learning task that is involved.

Uncertainty is obviously piled upon uncertainty in making contrastive analyses. Such uncertainties arise from inadequacies in existing linguistic theories. As an example of theoretical inadequacy, one may observe that the notion of deep structure itself is extremely uncertain. Chomsky (1968), McCawley (1968), and Fillmore (1968) all mean somewhat different things by it, but all at least agree that it has something to do with meaning. However, for the purposes of contrastive analysis any claim that all languages are very much the same at the level of deep structure seems to be little more than a claim that it is possible to talk about the same things in all languages, which is surely not a very interesting claim, except perhaps in that it seems to contradict the one made by Sapir and Whorf. The preceding statement is not meant to be a criticism of generative-transformational theory; it is meant to show how acceptance of that theory can fairly easily lead one to reject the idea that it is possible to make contrastive analyses, or, put less strongly, to reject the idea that generative-transformational theory has something to contribute to a theory of contrastive analysis, given the present state of the art.

Many experienced teachers find themselves unable to accept such reasons for rejection of the hypothesis. Their experience tells them that a Frenchman is likely to pronounce English *think* as *sink* and a Russian likely to pronounce it as *tink*, that a Spaniard will almost certainly fail to differentiate English *bit* from *beat*, and that an Englishman learning French will tend to pronounce the French word *plume* as *pleem* or *ploom*. They admit that in each case they must be prepared to teach the whole of the second language to a learner, but also insist that some parts of that second language are easier to learn than others, for no one ever must learn *everything* about the second language. However, many also admit that they do not know in what order learners should try to overcome the various difficulties they are observed to have. Should a Spaniard learning English learn to differentiate *bit* from *beat* and *bet* from *bait* because of the important surface contrasts which he does not make in Spanish? Or should he learn to associate the vowels in such pairs of words as *weep* and *wept, pale* and *pallid, type* and *typical, tone* and *tonic, deduce* and *deduction* so that he can somehow internalize the underlying phonological system of English? The mind boggles at this last possibility! But it is one which descriptions of Spanish and English based on generative-transformational theory would seem to hold out for teachers.

Some recent suggestions for using generative-transformational theory in contrastive analysis have actually been attempts to bring powerful theoretical insights to bear within the weaker version of the hypothesis in order to explain observed interference phenomena, for example some interesting work by Ritchie (1968) and by Carter (unpublished). In their work, Ritchie and Carter have used distinctive feature hierarchies in attempts to explain such problems as why a Russian is likely to say *tink* and a Frenchman *sink* for English *think*. Such work using the notions of feature hierarchy, rule-cycling, and morpheme-structure and word-structure rules has considerable possibilities. Certainly this kind of work seems more promising than some being done by others in an attempt to show gross similarities between deep structures in an assortment of languages.

5.0 Conclusion

In conclusion, it is fair to say that teachers of second or foreign languages are living in very uncertain times. A decade or so ago contrastive analysis was still a fairly new and exciting idea apparently holding great promise for teaching and curriculum construction. Now, one is not so sure—and not solely as a result of the Chomskyan revolution in linguistics. The contrastive-analysis hypothesis has not proved to be workable, at least not in the strong version in which it was originally expressed. This version can work only for one who is prepared to be quite naive in linguistic matters. In its weak version, however, it has proved to be helpful and undoubtedly will continue to be so as linguistic theory develops. However, the hypothesis probably will have less influence on second-language teaching and on course construction in the next decade than it apparently has had in the last decade.

This article was reprinted from *TESOL Quarterly*, Vol. 4, No. 2, by permission of the author and publishers. This is a slightly revised version of the paper which appeared in the *TESOL Quarterly*.

REFERENCES

Banathy, Bela, Edith Crowell Trager and Carl D. Waddle. "The Use of Contrastive Data in Foreign Language Course Development." *Trends in Language Teaching*, ed. A. Valdman. New York: McGraw-Hill, 1966, 27-56.

Carter, Richard J. "An Approach to a Theory of Phonetic Difficulties in Second-Language Learning." Bolt Beranek and Newman Inc., Report No. 1575.

Chomsky, Noam. *Language and Mind.* New York: Harcourt, Brace & World, 1968.

———, and Morris Halle. *The Sound Pattern of English.* New York: Harper and Row, 1968.

Fillmore, Charles J. "The Case for Case." *Universals in Linguistic Theory*, eds. E. Bach and R. T. Harms. New York: Holt, Rinehart and Winston, 1968, 1-88.

Fries, Charles C. *Teaching and Learning English as a Foreign Languages.* Ann Arbor: University of Michigan Press, 1945.

Lado, Robert. *Linguistics Across Cultures*. Ann Arbor: University of Michigan Press, 1957.

McCawley, James D. "The Role of Semantics in a Grammar." *Universals in Linguistic Theory*, eds. E. Bach and R.T. Harms. New York: Holt, Rinehart, and Winston, 1968, 124-169.

Ritchie, William C. "Some Implications of Generative Grammar for the Construction of Courses in English as a Foreign Language." *Language Learning*, 17 (1967), 45-69, 111-131.

———. "On the Explanation of Phonic Interference." *Language Learning*, 18 (1968), 183-197.

Schane, Sanford A. *French Phonology and Morphology*. Cambridge, Massachusetts: M.I.T. Press, 1968.

Stockwell, Robert P. and J. Donald Bowen. *The Sounds of English and Spanish*. Chicago: University of Chicago Press, 1965.

———, and John W. Martin. *The Grammatical Structures of English and Spanish*. Chicago: University of Chicago Press, 1965.

Weinreich, Uriel. *Languages in Contact: Findings and Problems*. New York: Linguistic Circle of New York, 1953.

Wolfe, David L. "Some Theoretical Aspects of Language Learning and Language Teaching." *Language Learning*, 17, (1967), 173-188.

C.
STUDENTS' ERRORS AND THE LEARNING OF FRENCH AS A SECOND LANGUAGE: A PILOT STUDY

MAGDELHAYNE F. BUTEAU

1.0 *Introduction*

The significance of students' errors seems to receive growing attention in psycholinguistic literature. Its relevance to Chomsky's (1965) duality theory of competence and performance and, more particularly, its relatedness to the objectives of Contrastive Linguistics make it a worthwhile area of investigation.

It is generally admitted that the various branches of Linguistics have had a promoting influence on foreign language pedagogy; but Contrastive Study appears to be more closely associated with the planning of textbook and curriculum content so as to obviate and remedy interference from native language habits. However, the predicting power of contrastive analysis is now seriously questioned; it is being confronted with approaches that are more directly concerned with pupil performance. Corder (1967) proposes the hypothesis that errors are evidence of the learners' strategies rather than signs of inhibition and he advocates a systematic study of errors in order to discover the learners' built-in syllabus. He claims that this information would be useful in many ways to textbook writers, teachers, and learners. Dušková (1969) investigated the sources of errors made by Czech students enrolled in an English course and tried to evaluate the importance of native language interference in the learning of a second language. Her findings partially support Wilkins' (1968) opinion: they suggest that students' errors are traceable not only to mother tongue patterns but also, among other factors, to confusion between forms and functions of the language being learnt. On the other hand, they do not justify Wilkins' claim that contrastive studies can be replaced entirely by an error-based analysis in determining the main areas of potential difficulty in second language learning. They also seem to contradict Nickel and Wagner (1968) who argue that contrastive analysis is sufficient and that consequently it should take priority over any other approaches. Like Politzer (1963) and Lado (1957), Dušková takes a mitigated stand and concludes that contrastive analysis might profitably be supplemented by the results of error-based analysis in the preparation of adequate teaching materials. More recently, James (1969), after expressing the opinion that Contrastive Study is "in the doldrums", insists on the urgency of undertaking serious heuristic investigation in order to test the predicting reliablility of Contrastive Study in second language teaching.

This article proposes to report data obtained from an enquiry about the errors made in a French grammar test, by 124 First Year College Entrants who presented the characteristics listed in Table I. There were 88 female students and 36 male students and their ages ranged from 16 to 20. The four groups were formed according to the languages spoken at home. The last group comprised students of various linguistic origins that were put together due to their small numbers.

Table 1. Student Characteristics and Achievement in French Grammar

Linguistic Background	Number of Subjects	Years of Fr. Study	H.S. General Average	Grammar Errors			
				Mean	S.D.	"t"	L. of sign.
1. *English Only*							
No Latin	29	7.00	68.8	18.17	7.81	.42	N.S.
With Latin	36	7.06	70.1	17.48	5.21		
2. *Engl. & French*							
No Latin	9	8.77	73.0	7.56	7.35	1.43	N.S.
With Latin	15	8.80	72.3	4.53	3.03		
3. *Engl. & Italian*							
No Latin	4	8.00	73.7	13.75	11.29	1.94	0.10
With Latin	21	6.90	73.7	8.33	3.43		
4. *Engl. & Other L.*							
No Latin	3	8.3	68.3	12.66	4.73	0.80	N.S.
With Latin	7	6.6	73.2	15.71	5.74		
TOTAL	124	7.4	71.2	13.47	7.8		

Polish	3	Dutch	1	
Hungarian	2	Greek	1	
Ukrainian	2	Lithuanian	1	

The grammar test that provided the corpus had been prepared primarily to supplement oral interviews held by the French Department for assigning candidates to the different First Year courses. It was made up of two parts. The first one contained forty-nine multiple-choice items taken from the French grammar program taught in *Parlons Francais I* (30) and *Parlons Francais II* (19) which are the official textnooks for the teaching of French in the Catholic high schools of the Province. Thirty-eight items corresponded to categories listed in the First Level of *Le Francais fondamental.* Table II shows the classification of the grammatical content from a contrastive point of view with English. It is to be noted that the 49 items have been converted into 63 cases because some items presented more than one problem, e.g., *Je visite le Canada.*

Table 2. Classification of Grammar Content

English-French Comparison / Categories	Parallel	Contrasting		
		Different	(0 English) (+ French)	(+ English) (0 French
Word Order	2	4	–	–
Forms and Inflections	4	12	17	–
Structure Words	6	9	7	2
TOTAL	12	25	24	2

The second part consisted of a free-expression exercise designed to test students' proficiency in the correct use of verbal forms in past, present, and future situations. The examinees were asked to write a short note (about 100-150 words) on each one of the following topics.

A   *Un accident dont j'ai été témoin.*
B   *L'importance de l'instruction.*
C   *Ce que je ferai l'été prochain.*

2.0 *Results and Comments*

Part One

1. No question was correctly or incorrectly answered by the whole group. No one had all questions right. Two students, both French-speaking, had only one error, and nine students had more than 25 errors. These summary considerations and the data listed in Table III, which are in agreement with Morrison's (1962) opinion that grade point average correlates with foreign language achievement, suggest the degree of validity of the test level, in the absence of any other criteria.

2. Table I data show that the study of Latin does not significantly correlate with achievement in French grammar, but it is to be noted that the mean number of errors of the first three groups is less for the subgroups who studied Latin and yet there is no evidence from High School General Averages that those who studied Latin were better achievers.

Table 3. Comparison of Extreme Groups

Group	N	Linguistic Background				Range of Errors	Mean H.S. Gen. Av.
		English Only	English and French	English and Italian	English and Other		
First Quartile	29	1	23	5	–	1–7	75.4
Fourth Quartile	31	27	1	1	2	20–33	69.3

3. In analyzing difficulty, four levels were established with the assumption that the difficulty of an item is inversely proportional to the percentage of success obtained on that item.

4. The six most difficult items correctly answered by only 42% or less are given in Table IV.
From the point of view of grammatical content, these items are distributed as follows:

Relative pronoun: form or/and inflection, structural function   3
Interrogative pronoun: form and inflection   1
Past participle: form and inflection   1
Infinitive Past: form and inflection   1

Table 4. Items Showing Low Success

Item	Distribution of Responses			
46. Prenez tout . . . vous avez besoin.	ce dont 26	ce que 91	ce qui 6	ce à quoi 1
45. C'est une maison . . . il faudra faire des réparations.	à laquelle 30	dont 50	qu' 31	de laquelle 11
19. . . . de ces histoires ces jeunes filles ont-elles écoutées avec le plus d'attention?	lesquelles 31	laquelle 58	auxquelles 26	desquelles 9
20. Voici les deux arbres à l'ombre . . . nous nous sommes reposés.	desquels 52	dont 58	duquelle 7	de laquelle 6
36. Après . . ., la vendeuse est revenue à son comptoir.	s'être reposée 53	se reposant 27	s'avoir reposée 25	se reposer 19
49. Voici les deux belles pommes que Jean . . . dans le panier pour toi.	a mises 53	a mis 66	a metté 5	mettées 0

Only item No. 45 involves a parallel structure: it can be rendered word for word in English and gender agreement is not here part of the problem. But all six items revolve around relational functions which are not included in the First Level of *Le Francais fondamental*. The error trend shows incomplete or missing structural concord and can be traced back to lack of understanding of the functional relationship within the French sentence. The use of the present participle after the preposition *aprés* is evidently related to English pattern; it is not surprising that 21 of the 27 errors of this type were made by students who speak English only. Errors in the past participle agreement and in the use of *dont* are common among French native speakers (Frei, 1929); of the 24 French-speaking candidates, 9 and 12, respectively, had errors in these two items. Consequently, since all six items involved functional relationships that needed to be identified by native French speakers as well as others, before a correct choice of form could be made, it can be inferred that the delineation of such relationships is a more important factor of learning difficulty than mother tongue interference.

5. If we examine the eight items that appear at the second maximal level of difficulty, that is, that were answered correctly by more than 50% but less than 66% of the students, we note that they are equivalent from the point of view of frequency of usage *(Le Francais fondamental)* but that they present a great variety of cases: sequence of tenses after *aussitôt que,* use of determiners, type and form of pronouns, prepositions, verbal inflection and comparison. Two may be considered as presenting parallel structures in the two languages. High error frequency reflects analogy with English in four instances: the present tense after *aussitôt que,* the omission of a determiner with *Canada,* the use of *chague* instead of *chacun,* and the preposition system with *demander.* As for the remaining items, they show error consistency originating from confusion within the French system of rules, e.g., *ils finissont, chacuns, c'est difficile* referring to a preceding noun, etc. This type of error seems to support Corder's opinion that some errors provide evidence of the learner's analogic patterns.

6. At the end of the difficulty scale, there were sixteen items that were presumably found easier, since they were correctly answered by at least more than 80% of the group. They could all be considered as non-parallel when compared with their English versions. Here are a few observations:

a) Contrasting word order patterns seem to be easier than parallel ones: *Je ne la trouve pas* was correctly answered by 120, whereas, *invitez-les* was chosen by 91 only. This result does not agree with Politzer's (1968) conclusion.

b) The low incidence of error in the eight cases of verbal forms would suggest that inflection is easier to learn than the proper use of tenses, independently of the dissimilarity of the two linguistic systems.

c) The type of incorrect responses shows the influence of English in eight of the sixteen cases; the others look like wrong choices within possible French options. For instance, *la mienne est vert* can be associated with the English absence of adjectival agreement, but *je n'ai pas des livres* could simply be a case of overgeneralization in the use of determiners in French.

The general findings of this summary error-survey seem to indicate that the French sentences that correspond literally to their English equivalents are not necessarily the easiest to learn, that the probability of errors could not be assessed only from the degree of divergence of the two linguistic structures, and consequently other factors of difficulty must be hypothesized.

Part Two: Free Expression

This report will deal only with the aspect of consistency of error noted in the short essays that the students had to write.

1. About 85% of the students made the same kind of error in their compositions and in the objective test. The consistency of error concerned only 20% of the 63 cases that were found in the test. The highest degree of correspondence appeared in the preposition system, gender and number agreement, and the use of determiners.

2. Within the free-expression exercise only, high incidence of error was found in gender distinction. Nearly 65% of the students confused noun genders in five or more instances. This observation supports Tucker, Lambert, and Rigault's (1969) findings about the difficulty that learners of French have with gender identification of French nouns.

3. Comparison of errors made by students with different linguistic background revealed no significant difference, except for French-speaking students. Those who speak Italian or another language showed about the same instances of English interference and of confusion with other French forms as those who speak English only. Moreover, there was not particular within-group consistency that would suggest marked interference from Italian or other languages. The apparent absence of mother tongue traces may be justified by the fact that all these students had received their schooling in an English-language system.

3.0 Discussion of Results and Conclusions

In the test under study, there are a number of environmental factors that could have influenced individual students in their choices, namely, the form and the order of the different alternatives within the list of the four possibilities, the semantic elements of each statement, the frequency of usage in oral and written communication, the relative teaching emphasis given to each item, etc. But it may reasonably be assumed that these factors were about neutralized by the variety of traits, of the First Year College Entrants that served as subjects. I shall then proceed to a more detailed analysis of the errors and reexamine their correspondence with the concept of similarity as a correlate of transfer in second-language learning.

I propose that, for native speakers of English who are at the intermediate level in their study of French, the concept of similarity has to be considered internally, from the point of view of the French subsystems, as well as externally, from a comparative point of view with English. Moreover, it seems realistic to assume that the greater the extension of a generalization, the more easily it is learned and applied, because it embraces a large number of similar cases, as, for instance, the subject-verb sequence that is generally found both in French and in English statements. On the contrary, the manipulation of particular rules calls for the discrimination of cues and identification of categories, such as kind of sentence, group of verb, type of pronoun, nature of function, direction of relationship, etc. It becomes a problem-solving situation involving different levels of choices concerning elements whose similarity with what has been learnt before has to be clearly perceived. An incorrect response may be interpreted as a wrong choice resulting from improper generalization, confusion of cues, or, in the absence of perceived signals, conscious or unconscious recourse to imitation of native language patterns. The last case is usually considered as an instance of interference. This theory of choice seems to be in agreement with Carroll's (1966) suggestion that the learning of grammar in foreign languages occurs through some sort of internalized process that at least at some stage is guided consciously. But this guidance which makes up for the factors of extensive contact and pressing motivation that usually accompany first language acquisition must imply nuclei from which similarity networks can be organized so as to facilitate choices and strategies. Besides, the learner needs signs that will help him make proper decisions. If French is presented to him as a self-contained system, he will be less tempted to refer constantly to his native language for a model or for clues. For instance, if he wishes to tell someone to invite his friends, his subconscious or conscious framework of reference should not be that this is a case where English and French use the same word order, but that a positive command in French is a minority instance that calls for the postposition of the object pronoun. However, this in no way denies that second-language grammar learning can be facilitated by native language, particularly in the aspects where the two systems are basically congruent, as, for example, word order. Here, French and English are similar in their dependence on this structural device to express certain relationships. The learning set developed in using word order in English facilitates the acquisition. Moreover, the second-language learner who has internalized certain basic segments of his new linguistic system will use his native language acquisition device *(lad)* to work out, from this new "primary matter", generalizations that are comparable to those of a native speaker of French. For instance, *Prêtez-moi-la* was chosen by many, including some French-speaking students. This error which can hardly be attributed to English interference reflects French overgeneralization. Due to the much wider use of a single object pronoun and the constant adjunction of the strong pronoun *moi* with positive command, independently of the nature of the complement involved, French speakers and even learners of French, are influenced by these environmental factors and induced into a faulty extension of this pattern when there are two pronouns involved.

Similarly, if we compare *je ne la trouve pas* and *invitez-les,* we find that the former involves greater generalization in French than the latter and, as such, would be easier to learn. This was substantiated in our findings by a statistically significant difference of 29 correct answers.

Intralinguistic interference also occurs frequently in morphology (Dušková). In such cases, generalization may be played out by other factors. Concerning verbal forms, teaching emphasis may create special awareness of subsystem cues and thus facilitate proper choices in dealing with minority cases. This opinion was supported by the responses observed in the following three items:

No. 1.	*Ces étudiants attendent:*	118		No. 28.	*Tes amis viennent:*	113
	attendre:	2			*venont:*	7
	attendu:	4			*venir:*	1
	attender:	0			*ont venir:*	2

No. 23.	*Ces élèves finissent:*	73
	finent:	18
	finirent:	16
	finissont:	15

As the three verbs concerned are listed in *Le Français fondamental,* they should not have offered any semantic difficulty. Two features of these results are particularly significant: the trend of the incorrect answers and the number of correct answers.

First of all, very few students seem to have followed the English verbal non-inflectional pattern. The subject-verb relation was so close and French verbs are so generally inflected that there was no complicated choice involved. Those who incorrectly picked the *"ont"* ending erred in generalizing the inflection used in the present tense of *avoir, être, faire, aller,* and in the future of all verbs. The others assimilated *finir* with the majority of French verbs and overgeneralized present tense formation in French. As for the number of correct answers, the difference between *viennent* and *finissent* can be accounted for by considering the number of choices involved. According to the textbook in use, *venir* is still presented as forming with *tenir* and their compounds a marginal group and, as such, is given amplified importance. On the other hand, *finir* is treated as a member of a class of verbs having a particular system of inflection. As *finissent* called for the double choice of class and system, it was not learned so easily as *viennent,* by the subjects of this test.

The relation of difficulty and awareness of subsystems also finds relevance in the learning of French pronouns, as illustrated in two items dealing with the correct form of pronoun in expressions of possession.

No. 21. *Ces souliers blancs sont*
   ceux de ma soeur: 74
      celles: 32
       ces: 9
    ceux-lui: 9

No. 33. *Paul aime mieux ma cravate*
   que la sienne: 107
     le sien: 13
      sa: 3
      son: 1

Further analysis showed that 68 candidates answered both items correctly and that only three chose the correct pronoun form but the wrong agreement for the two items. As these two groups represent only 57% of all the candidates, it may then be inferred that this pair of items shows little consistency of error. It must also be noted that both items contain a problem of agreement and a choice between the French adjective and pronoun forms which have only one English equivalent: those, *ceux, ces;* his, *la sienne, sa.* From the point of view of form, there were only slightly more errors in the demonstrative item than in the possessive. The agreement aspect shows wider discrepancy. Here agreement depends on the choice of the term of reference and on the gender identification of this term. The gender of *ma cravate* is more clearly marked than that of *souliers blancs* which calls for an additional step in clue searching. Consequently, the greater difficulty of item 21 could be attributed to the greater number of clues required to arrive at the proper solution. However, it can hardly be inferred that possessives are necessarily easier to learn than demonstratives.

Errors in personal pronouns also give rise to different types of interference as evidenced in the following items which show small differences in correct answers but which were classified in different levels, in the above-mentioned four-degree difficulty scale. The slight difference in favor of the singular form might be justified by the fact that the word *lui* fills in more functions than *ceux* and its choice requires less discrimination. While signs of English analogy can be found in the choice of the subject pronoun in item 13, the errors in item 38 show confusion with French pronouns and unawareness of the signal given by the comparison.

According to Pascasio (1961) and Stockwell (1965), maximal degree of difficulty is encountered in the learning of grammar elements that do not exist in the native language. French gender agreement, which is a structural device that is not used in English, did not seem to present as high a degree of difficulty as predicted by these specialists. Responses were as follows:

No. 4.   *Ce chapeau est celui de Marie:*   94
                                  Cet: 17
                                Cette: 14
                                C'est: 0

No. 5. *Ta robe est rouge, la mienne est verte:*   111
                                        vert: 8
                                      vertée: 4
                                        vère: 1

The use of *vert* and *cette* seems to reflect unawareness of gender signals, but the use of *vert* could also result from non-agreement analogy with English. The use of *cet* indicates awareness of gender but confusion with the different forms of the demonstrative adjective. As gender agreement was achieved by nearly 90% of the group, the present findings lead us to consider that it may be counted among the easily internalized patterns of French in spite of its almost complete absence in English. This facility may be related to the generality of the phenomenon in French.

In conclusion, even if the above partial analysis is insufficient to justify completely the ordering of difficulty obtained from the results of the test under study, it provides enough evidence that error-based analyses are not only fruitful but also necessary to work out and test hypotheses concerning factors that set degrees of difficulty in second language learning at the intermediate level. Moreoever, on the assumption that grammar competence is essentially a matter of correct choices, this study can be considered as supporting the opinion that, from the point of view of linguistics, difficulty is a function of the number of possible alternatives involved, and, psychologically, from the point of view of the learner, difficulty is a function of the awareness of contextual cues.

Reprinted from *IRAL* Vol. 8, No. 2, by permission of the author and publisher.

REFERENCES

Carroll, John B.: "Research in Foreign Language Teaching: The Last Five Years", in Mead, R. G. (ed.): *Language Teaching: Broader Contexts.* Report of the Northeast Conference, 1966.

Chomsky, Noam: *Aspects of the Theory of Syntax.* Cambridge, Mass.: M.I.T. Press, 1965.

Corder, S.P.: "The Significance of Learners' Errors", *IRAL*, V, 4 (Nov. 1967),161-171.

Dušková, Libuše: "On Sources of Errors in Foreign Language Learning", *IRAL*, VII, 1 (Feb. 1969), 11-36.

Frei, Henri, *La Grammaire des fautes*, Paris: Geuthner, 1929.

James, Carl: "Deeper Contrastive Study", *IRAL*, VII, 2 (May 1969), 83-95.

Lado, Robert L.: *Linguistics Across Cultures.* Ann Arbor, Mich.: The University of Michigan Press, 1957.

Morrison, A.V.: "Personality and Under-Achievement in Foreign Language Learning", in Pimsleur, P., *Under-Achievement in Foreign Language Learning.* Ohio: Ohio State University Research Foundation, 1962.

Nickel, Gerhard and K. H. Wagner: "Contrastive Linguistics and Language Teaching", *IRAL*, VI, 3 (August 1968), 233-256.

Pascasio, Emy M.: "Predicting Interference and Facilitation for Tagalog Speakers in Learning English", *Language Learning*, XI, 1-2 (March 1961), 79-84.

Politzer, Robert, L.: "An Experiment in the Presentation of Parallel and Contrasting Structures", *Language Learning*, XVIII, 1-2 (June 1968), 35-43.

Politzer, Robert L., and Hagiwara, M.: *Active Review of French* (Preface). Toronto: Blasidell Publishing Co. 1963.

Stockwell, R. P., Bowen, J. Donald, and Martin, John W.: *The Grammatical Structures of English and Spanish.* Chicago: The University of Chicago Press, 1965.

Tucker, G. Richard, Lambert, W.E., and Rigault, A.: "Students' Acquisition of French Gender Distinctions: A Pilot Investigation", *IRAL*, VII, 1 (Feb. 1969), 51-55.

Whitmarsh, W.F.H., and Klinck, G.A.: *Parlons Français I & II.* Toronto: Longmans, Green and Company, 1957.

Wilkins, D.A.: "Review of A. Valdman (ed.), *Trends in Language Teaching*", *IRAL*, VI, 1 (Feb. 1968), 99-107.

d.
ERROR ANALYSIS
AND SECOND LANGUAGE STRATEGIES

JACK C. RICHARDS

The field of error analysis may be defined as dealing with the differences between the way people learning a language speak, and the way adult native speakers of the language use the language. Such differences may create interest for a variety of reasons. We may begin with the interests of those who study language "for its own sake." Since language is not simply a more complex instance of something found elsewhere in the animal world, Chomsky suggests that the study of human language is the most fruitful way of discovering what constitutes human intelligence. Some of the most insightful notions about what language is have come from observing how language is acquired by children. By looking at children's speech, comparing it with adult speech, and trying to account for the differences, psycholinguists have been able to speculate about the nature of the mental processes that seem to be involved in language.

While the mother-child relationship and other language-crucial activities of the child's experience do not include any consciously incorporated instructional strategies, in the field of second language teaching elaborate instructional procedures are often defended as being essential components in successful second language learning. Since the goal of the language course is to lead the learner toward adult uses of the new language, differences between the way the learner and the native speaker speak the language have been studied in the hope that methods of overcoming these difficulties might be devised. Errors in second language learning, it is sometimes said, could be avoided if we were to make a comparison of the learner's mother tongue and the target language. The sum of the differences would constitute his learning difficulties, and it is here that teaching strategies would be optimal. Alternatively, interpretation of errors in second language learning along the lines of errors in first language learning suggests that second language errors are not, by nature, different from those made by children learning English as a mother tongue, hence they should not be of undue concern to language teachers. The purpose of the present paper is to look at recent and less recent ideas on errors in second language learning, in the hope that such an examination might illuminate the experience of second language teachers.

1.0 "Errors in First Language Learning

What sort of ideas about language and language learning have been deduced from differences between children's and adult speech? Firstly, considerable support for current notions of language have been found in studies of child language development. It used to be thought that speaking was simply the exercise of our individual verbal habits, and that these were acquired through repetition, reinforcement, and conditioning, in much the same way as animals can be trained to perform certain tasks through the use of appropriate conditioning techniques. It is suggested that this is an inadequate account of language and of language learning. In children, it appears that the process of formulating language is an active and creative process, yet a process that follows similar patterns in children across quite differing learning circumstances. All children learning English as a mother tongue seem to follow a similar sequence in their acquisition of grammar, for instance. If we listen to the speech of English-speaking children at about three or four years old for example, we hear them using question forms like this (Bellugi, 1968):

What he can ride in?
Where I should put it?
Why he is doing it?

These questions share a common structural feature that makes them different from adult questions. In these questions, that part of the sentence that normally comes after the subject in the statement form—the *can* in *He can do it*—has been left in this position in the question form, instead of being put before the subject as in the adult sentence *What can he do?* Now at about the same time as children are producing sentences like this, they *are* able to make questions that do not require a *wh*-word such as *where* or *why*. They have no difficulty in saying *Can he ride in a truck?* but when they use a *wh*-word they fail to change the word order and produce *What he can ride in?*

It is clear from instances like this in children's language that the children are not simply imitating the speech of their parents, for sentences like this do not appear in adult speech. If we were to compare the sentences that the child is capable of producing at this stage with those of an adult, we would have an illustration of the child's *competence* at age three or four compared with adult competence.

Child's competence

He possesses the rules permitting questions with the form: *Can he go? Where he can go?*
He cannot produce: *Where can he go?*

Adult's competence

He possesses the rules permitting questions with the form: *Can he go? Where can he go?*

By looking at the differences between the child's sentences and those of the adult we see evidence of the way the child appears to be formulating hypotheses about the English language, some of which he will eventually abandon in favor of the rules of adult language. Since the differences between children's and adult speech are *systematic*, found wherever children learn English, psycholinguists have been able to postulate universals that seem to be crucial for language development (Slobin, 1970).

Now the crucial elements in first language acquisition would seem to center on the psychology of learning, that is, those strategies employed by the child as he teaches himself his mother tongue, the development of his other faculties such as intelligence, cognition, perception, and so on, and the structure and rules of the particular language he is acquiring, in this case, English. These would appear to shape and formulate the sentences he produces in a systematic way. It has been suggested that the differences between the way a second language is often spoken and the way the language is spoken by native speakers are systematic, just as children's language follows a definite norm and developmental sequence of its own, as we saw with the example of the use of questions. Corder believes that errors in second language speech reveal a systematic attempt to deal with the data, and that they should play the same role in our study of second language learning as differences between child and adult speech play in the study of first language acquisition. "It is in such an investigation that the study of learners' errors (in second language learning) would assume the role it already plays in the study of child language acquisition, since the key concept . . . is that the learner is using a definite system of language at every point in his development, although it is not the adult system in the one case, nor that of the second language in the other. The learner's errors are evidence of this system and are themselves systematic" (Corder, 1967).

2.0 *The Significance of Errors in Second Language Learning*

If learners' errors in second language acquisition are systematic, in what ways are they organized, and what do they suggest about the nature of second language acquisition? Selinker calls the speech output in a second language an *Interlanguage*, since it invariably differs from the target language, and he uses the term *fossilization* to refer to permanent characteristics of the speech of bilinguals irrespective of the age at which the second language is acquired or the amount of instruction or practice in it. He characterizes fossilization in the following way: "it is my contention that the most interesting phenomena in interlanguage performance are those items, rules and subsystems which are fossilizable. . . . If it can be experimentally demonstrated that fossilizable items, rules and subsystems which occur in interlanguage performance are a result of the native language then we are dealing with the process of *language transfer*, if these fossilizable items, rules and subsystems are a result of identifiable items in training procedures, then we are dealing with *transfer-of-training*, if they are a result of an identifiable approach by the learner to the material to be learned, then we are dealing with *strategies of learning*, if they are the result of an identifiable approach by the learner to communication with native speakers of the target language, then we are dealing with *strategies of communication*, and finally if they are the result of a clear overgeneralization of target language rules then we are dealing with the *reorganization of linguistic materials*. I would like to hypothesize that these five processes are central processes in second language learning and that each process forces fossilizable material upon surface Interlanguage utterances, controlling to a very large extent the shape of these utterances" (Selinker, 1969*a*, 1969*b*).

I should like to focus on Selinker's description of interlanguage characteristics as a basis for an account of typical errors in second language communication in English. As data I will begin with an analysis of samples of English speech elicited from two speakers, one whose mother tongue is European French, the other whose mother tongue is Czech. To obtain the six speech samples presented in Figure 1, the speakers were given a number of short texts in English; they were instructed to read the texts and then asked to relate the content of each text in their own words without referring to the texts. In what ways does their performance of this task illustrate systematic approaches to second language communication?

3.0 *Interference*

Perhaps some of the most apparent examples of fossilizable items in second language communication are those described as instances of language transfer or interference. This may be defined as the use of elements from one language while speaking another and may be found at the level of pronunciation, morphology, syntax, vocabulary, and meaning. Examples 1, 2, 3, 4, and 7 in Sample 1 for example, reflect the use of elements of French morphology and syntax. In Example 1, the plural -*s* is omitted, perhaps because plurals are not pronounced in French. A French structure is used in Example 2—*has allowed to capitalist man*—following the French structure—*a permis au capitaliste de*—. In Example 3, French article usage is reflected in the use of—*the money*—following the French—*pour investir l'argent*—. In Example 7, the influence of French likewise seems evident, *have the possibility to do great profits* follows the French—*ont la possibilité de faire de grands profits.*

These examples of interference might appear to confirm some of the claims that have sometimes been made for the possibility of predicting instances of interference by contrasting the grammatical or other systems of two languages. "We can predict and describe the patterns that will cause difficulty in learning and those that will not cause difficulty, by comparing systematically the language and culture to be learned with the language and culture of the student" (Lado, 1957). Many such contrasts between languages have been attempted, though they have been criticized because they make demands on linguistic theory that our present knowledge about language is simply not ready to meet. We do not know enough about the higher-level organization of particular languages to make the neat sort of contrasts that such statements imply either feasible or meaningful. Most of the contrasts that have been made have been based on practical knowledge of two languages rather than on any systematic application of a theory of contrastive analysis (see Wardhaugh, 1970). Yet the instances of interference we have looked at seem so evident that it might appear that second language data can be entirely described in such terms. Indeed it often has been. What happens in fact is that in analyzing second language data it is tempting to see all errors as effects of the interference of the mother tongue, ignoring all other relevant phenomena. Both Samples 1 and 2 provide examples of errors that require alternative interpretations.

Figure 1. Samples of Second Language Speech

Sample 1 (French)

The fact that land and minerals are very cheap in inaccessible *region*[1] and the development of new techniques *has allowed to capitalist man*[2] to invest *the money*[3] in this region and exploit *the minerals.*[4] It's . . . this *is occurs*[5] in Australia where man has exploited huge *mounting*[6] of minerals in this region. And they *have the possibility to do great profits*[7] in this part of the country.

1. Interference (plural not pronounced in French)
2. Interference (a permis au capitaliste de . . .)
3. Interference (l'argent)
4. Interference (les minéraux)
5. Overgeneralization
6. Overgeneralization
7. Interference (ont la possibilité de faire de grands profits)

Sample 2 (Czech)

In the first part of the article the *author give*[1] us reasons for investment in inaccessible regions. The reason for . . . to invest in *this regions*[2] is the *possibility to buy*[3] land, minerals and deposits at very low cost. Another factor which *permits to invest*[4] in this region is the development of new technology which *permits to connected*[5] *this inaccessible regions*[6] in *short time*[7] with the regional . . . the regions which are civilized.

1. Overgeneralization
2. Overgeneralization
3. Overgeneralization
4. Overgeneralization
5. Overgeneralization
6. Overgeneralization
7. Interference

Sample 3 (French)

The human eye may be compared to a camera. The camera functions with a lens . . . *would*[1] *enregistrate*[2] by a lens and a screen behind it which *enregistrate*[3,4] the image. Once the image is developed *it stay*[5] here. *In contrary*[6] in movies the image *disappear*[7] from the screen. The eye-human eye functions like . . . like the camera. It is *composed with*[8] a lens and behind the lens is *little*[9] screen coated with cells and *enregistrates*[10] the light.

1. Performance error
2. Interference (French borrowing)
3. Interference (French borrowing)
4. Overgeneralization (Omission of -s)
5. Overgeneralization
6. Interference (au contraire)
7. Overgeneralization
8. Overgeneralization
9. Performance error
10. Interference (French borrowing)

Sample 4 (Czech)

The author of the article compares the function of a camera and the function of the human eye. In an ordinary camera we have *lens*[1] which *concentrate*[2] beams of light on the film which is in the back of *camera.*[3] This light *can impress the film and in this way to fix*[4] the image of the film. The function of the human eye is very similar. We have the same lens in our eye and the film which is found in *camera*[5] is replaced in our eye by *retina,*[6] an organic matter which is *composed by*[7] light sensitive cells.

1. Interference
2. Overgeneralization
3. Interference
4. Performance error
5. Interference
6. Interference
7. Overgeneralization

Sample 5 (French)

Steam engine[1] is *composed with*[2] a cylinder in which a piston can move easily and which *fix*[3] *well the cylinder.*[4] This piston is *actionated*[5] by the steam and it is connected to a wheel

1. Performance error
2. Overgeneralization
3. Overgeneralization
4. Interference (fixe bien le cylindre)
5. Interference (actionné)

which it *makes turned.*[6] The steam ... this engine *has been discovered*[7] in the 18th century, but James Watt is the person who *ameliorate*[8] it and who *give*[9] it *his actual form.*[10]

6. Interference (le fait tourner)
7. Interference (a été découvert)
8. Interference (French borrowing)
9. Performance error
10. Interference (sa forme actuelle)

Sample 6 (Czech)

The article is about the invention of *steam machine.*[1] *Steam machine*[2] was invented in *17th century*[3] by an Englishman, James Watt. The principle of the steam machine is ... the basis of the steam machine is *piston*[4] which is pushed by the pressure of *steam.*[5] This piston is *connected with*[6] a wheel by a rod and in this way the motion of the wheel is possible.

1. Interference
2. Interference
3. Interference
4. Interference
5. Interference
6. Overgeneralization

4.0 *Overgeneralization*

In Samples 1 and 2 we find examples of a similar type of error, illustrated by *this is occurs* (Example 5 in Sample 1) and *the author give us* (Example 1 in Sample 2). Here we have a similar type of error from both the French and Czech subjects. These illustrate what Selinker calls overgeneralization of target language rules, or the reorganization of linguistic materials. Jakobovits (1970: 111-12) defines generalization as "the use of previously available strategies in new situations. ... In second language learning some of these strategies will prove helpful in organizing the facts about the second language, but others, perhaps due to superficial similarities will be misleading and inapplicable." In Sample 1 the French speaker seems to have generalized the form *is occurs* from his experience of forms like *it is made of* and *it occurs*. In the Czech example in Sample 2 the omission of the third person -*s* in *the author give us* may result from the pressure of other forms in English without *s*. Dušková (1969) remarks, "Since (in English) all grammatical persons take the same zero verbal ending except for the third person singular in the present tense . . . omissions of the -*s* in the third person singular in the present tense may be accounted for by the heavy pressure of all the other endingless forms. The endingless form is generalized for all persons."

These examples of overgeneralization are the effects of particular learning strategies on items within the target language, and since such learning strategies appear to be universally employed when a learner is exposed to second language data, it is not surprising that many of the errors found in second language communication are identical despite the background language of the speaker. The elements that differ are those effects of language transfer or interference while those that we find in common are the results of other learning strategies. One aspect of generalization has often been referred to in studies of first language acquisition. It has frequently been remarked that children learning English as their mother tongue will produce forms like *comed*, and *goed*, by analogy with past tense formation in regular verbs. Among children acquiring French as their mother tongue we likewise find things such as *on poudra* instead of *on pourra* (we will be able . . .) by probable analogy with *on voudra* (see Kinzel, 1964). Likewise both French-speaking children and people learning French as a second-language produce sentences like *je serai très malcontent* instead of *je serai très mécontent* presumably on the analogy:

> *heureuse/malheureuse   content/malcontent*

Similar processes seem to account for common preposition mistakes in English. The pressure of one English construction on another as the learner tests out his hypotheses about the structure of English may account for forms like *permits to invest* and *permits to connected* in Sample 2 and the other examples of overgeneralization by analogy noted in the other samples. (Sample 1, Example 6; Sample 2, Example 3, 4, and 5; Sample 3, Example 8; Sample 4, Example 7; Sample 5, Example 2; Sample 6, Example 6).

In Sample 3 we have an interesting demonstration that the French speaker is not simply transferring the grammar of his mother tongue into English. In Example 8 he uses *composed with* instead of *composed of*. The Czech speaker in Sample 4, Example 7, likewise uses *composed by* and in Sample 5, Example 2, the French speaker again produces *composed with* instead of *composed of*. Had the French speaker followed the grammar of his mother tongue here he would have produced the correct English form. In French the equivalent would be *composé de* which is the English equivalent of *composed of*. The French equivalent of the form the French speaker used (*composé avec*) would in fact be inappropriate in French in this context. Both the French and the Czech speaker are evidently trying to work out the particular rules of English structure, being guided here not by the grammar of the mother tongue but by what they already know of English, and by their own intuitions. As Wolfe (1967) comments: "Once the student grasps the idea that the new language differs from his native language in many matters of structure, he will not know when it is safe to operate in terms of his native language (it seldom is) and he may try to create his own structures on the basis of previous contact with the new language. . . . Some students, not knowing a correct form, will make up a form which does not parallel either the native or the target language. Or a student will persistently fail to make a grammatical distinction in the target language which he actually does make in his mother tongue." We see examples of this from the French speaker, who fails to use the past tense in Sample 5, Example 9, although this would be required were he recounting the text in French. The psychological parameters in second language learning thus cannot be identified exclusively with the linguistic ones.

The effect of rules within the target language has been described in more formal terms by Falk in this way: "Few if any of the rules of the syntactic component are completely independent of the other rules. The formulation of one rule will invariably affect other rules in the grammar. . . . Because this is so, the construction of a subgrammar, i.e., of some subset of the rules for a particular language, is a complicated task. Some of the rules in such a subgrammar will inevitably be ad hoc since the limited nature of the undertaking excludes detailed consideration of all the linguistic facts which may affect the rules" (Falk, 1968).

So far I have talked about interference and overgeneralization as if they were independent factors. The facts are not quite so consistent. In Samples 4 and 6 the Czech speaker consistently omits articles, and this I have attributed to interference, since articles are not present in his mother tongue. Dušková (1969:18) notes, however, "Although the difficulty in mastering the use of articles in English is ultimately due to the absence of this grammatical category in Czech, once the learner starts internalizing their system, interference from all the other terms of the (English) article system begins to operate as an additional factor." This no doubt leads to diffidence and hesitancy in the use of articles by the Czech speaker.

5.0 *Performance Errors*

If language learning both in a first and second language setting involves trying out hypotheses about the language from one's experience of it (and in the case of second language learning, from one's experience of other languages), and abstracting the rules that permit us to produce sentences in the language, then we shall need to go further than looking at simple examples of interference, overgeneralization, and analogy. These processes are in themselves insufficient to account for the complexity of language learning. The samples we have looked at do not enable us to say whether these mistakes are occasional, or represent permanent states in the speaker's competence. In Sample 3 for instance, the speaker says (Example 9) *behind the lens is little screen*, omitting the article. But what does this error really represent? There are several possibilities. First, we may exclude interference from the mother tongue, since this would have required the use of the article in French. A second possibility is that the speaker realized the mistake as he said it but forgot to correct it—that he would have corrected it if he had had more time to think about it. In fact when looking at the transcribed text the speaker did correct this mistake himself.

Now this is something that the child who says *What he can ride in?* is unable to do. The child's competence is represented by that particular sentence, whereas this particular article error by the French speaker is simply the sort of error anyone is likely to make speaking under normal circumstances. It is therefore an error at the level of *performance* rather than competence. Performance errors are quite normal aspects of language use. When we are tired or hurried, we all make errors of this type. There is a similar error in Sample 4, Example 4. The Czech speaker was able to recognize the mistake in *This light can impress the film and in this way to fix the image of the film*. This error was probably a function of the length of the sentence the speaker was trying to produce, hence it is related to memory limitations rather than to competence. Clearly if we want to have a more certain idea of someone's competence in a second language, we need to take a much closer and more detailed look at his speech output to find out if his sentences consistently display particular interlanguage characteristics, that is, to find out if the speaker has internalized a system of some sort that does not correspond to that of the native speaker.

6.0 *Markers of Transitional Competence*

Just as we need to be able to distinguish between performance and competence errors in the analysis of second language data, so it may be necessary to distinguish between those errors that indicate the learning sequence by which particular grammatical rules are built up, and those that represent the final state of the speaker's competence. In our example of first language learning for example, sentences like *What he can ride in?* seem to be produced by all English speaking children before they are able to use the form of the adult grammar—*What can he ride in?* Are some of the errors observed in second language learning also representative of developmental sequences by means of which the learner masters the rules of the

English grammatical system? This question cannot be answered from the data I have presented here, and I know of no studies that could confirm or reject such a hypothesis. What is needed are detailed longitudinal studies of an adult learner's progress with a second language, documenting the appearance and development of particular structures. The types of short-term errors attributed here to overgeneralization and analogy could then be placed within the overall sequence of language development. It may be that the innate ability to generate and hypothesize rules, so evident in first language acquisition, becomes subordinate in adult second language learning to secondary learning strategies, such as generalization, borrowing, and memorization, for purely biological reasons. It should also be noted that I am using terms like interference, analogy, and generalization, without relating them to a psycholinguistic model of language. They are used here simply as convenient ways of classifying observable phenomena at the level of speech, though this does not explain how they are represented at the level of language. Psycholinguistic models (such as that of Jakobovits, 1970: chapter 4) have been proposed that do try to account for such factors as interference and generalization.

If we were to try to locate our Czech speaker's article errors at the level of competence, we would require a close developmental study of his article usage as he acquires English, to find out if after some exposure to English, his use of articles was entirely haphazard, or whether he had worked out some consistent way of dealing with them. Is his learning task the same as that of the child faced with the appearance of articles in his mother tongue?

Jones (1970), in his study of child language development, places the development of the article system as coming logically and necessarily after the development of the substantive or noun. It is a further conceptualization of the substantive, permitting a point of view that conceptualizes it either as a universal or a particular. Leopold (1939-) found that articles were not used at all by his child subject in the first two years but later took on systematic usage. With an adult acquiring the system as a second language, however, cognitive development has already occurred, hence he may have to resort to other strategies to develop rules to deal with the article system in English.

7.0 *Other Forms of Interference*

Before looking at other aspects of second language learning strategies, I should like to refer to an aspect of interference that is not manifest in the particular samples we have looked at so far, but which is nevertheless quite widespread. This has to do with contrasts between styles across languages. We may regard style as the choice we have within a language of a particular mode of expression, such as formal or informal, and colloquial or officious. In some speech communities differences of this sort are so marked and have become so institutionalized that they may be regarded as quite distinct varieties of the same language. In Baghdad, according to Ferguson (1959), the Christian Arabs speak a "Christian Arabic" dialect when talking among themselves but speak a general Baghdad dialect "Muslim Arabic" when talking in a mixed group. This phenomenon, where two distinct varieties of a language exist side by side in a community, with each having a definite and distinct role to play, is what Ferguson called *diglossia*. What typically happens is that particular functions are assigned to each variety of the language, the most fundamental distinction being between what may be called High and Low uses of the language. The High form is generally regarded as superior to the Low form and is compulsory for certain types of situations. Ferguson gives sample situations, with indications of the appropriate form of the language to be used:

sermon in church or mosque	H	
instructions to servants, waiters, clerks, workmen		L
personal letter	H	
speech in Parliament	H	
university lecture	H	
conversation with family, friends, colleagues		L
news broadcast	H	
radio soap opera		L
newspaper editorial, news story, caption on picture	H	
caption on political cartoon		L
poetry	H	
folk literature		L

Now the differences between the High and Low forms of languages that exhibit this phenomenon, and it is very widespread—Arabic, Modern Greek, Swiss German, and many Asian languages for example—are much greater than those between what we may call a formal or informal style in English. In diglossic communities the High style may have striking differences in grammar and in word order, and in the area of the vocabulary the High style may have a much more learned and classical lexicon than the Low.

People who belong to language communities that manifest this phenomenon may come to expect such switching between distinct language varieties to be a universal feature of languages. In other words, when they come to write something in English that would demand a high style in their mother tongue, they may feel a pressure to give their English a correspondingly high style. Thus one finds people who write English clearly and faultlessly, exhibiting what I call "diglossamania" in certain situations. In English for example, we do not feel that there is a low status about words of high frequency, in the vocabulary we use in normal everyday situations. A Tamil-speaking student however may prefer the feel of *I instructed him to obtain it for me* over *I told him to get it for me.* There may be a distinct preference for archaic words or for words of low frequency, whereas the native speaker of English prefers a simple style. You may have noticed this in written English from Greek or Arabic students, for example, depending on the topic they choose to write about.

The effects of the High/Low distinction in the student's mother tongue may also be evident at the grammatical level in his written English. Kaplan, in a 1967 article dealing with composition difficulties of Arab students, remarks that Arab students appear to prefer certain devices of conjoining sentences over others, thus the sentences:

The boy was here.
He drank the milk.

may be more frequently conjoined with *and* by Arab students, producing *The boy was here and he drank the milk* in preference to *The boy who was here drank the milk.* (See also Macmillan, 1970:146). This may be attributed to the influence of the grammar of a high style in Arabic. This use of balancing devices to create a more aesthetic style produces among certain Indian students sentences like:

While I am still a student, and yet I still have plenty of time.
Whenever I see him, then I feel happy.
Even though I am poor, yet I am happy.

Here are two examples from a letter-writing manual for students of English written by an Asian with a diglossic mother tongue. As a model for a personal letter he uses a distinctly high style:

With the warm and fragrant breath of Spring, here approaches the bliss of Eastertide. May it shower joy and happiness upon you all. The tide brings to my mind the old memories of several Easters feted with you and the decorated eggs placed on my dresser.

For an order however, the writer presents a normal low style as a model:

I want to order from you a copy of the latest edition of ___ book. In this connection please let me know what will be the total cost.

The prevalence of artificially high style uses of English among Indians has been called "Babu English" and it is well parodied in a novel by F. Anstey (1902):

After forming my resolution of writing a large novel, I confided it to my crony, Mr. Ram Ashootosh Lall, who warmly recommended to persevere in such a magnus opus. So I became divinely inflated periodically every evening from 8 to 12 p.m., disregarding all entreaties from feminine relatives to stop and indulge in a blow-out on ordinary eatables . . . and at length my colossal effusion was completed, and I had written myself out: after which I had the indescribable joy and felicity to read my composition to my mothers in law and wives and their respective progenies and offsprings, whereupon, although they were not acquainted with a word of English, they were overcome by such severe admiration for my fecundity and native eloquence that they swooned with rapture. . . .

In examining instances of interference or language transfer we thus need to consider more than just the linguistic variables and their distribution across languages; we need also to consider social reactions to different aspects of language use, since these too may be carried from one language to another, influencing the sort of sentences that may be formulated in the second language.

8.0 *Strategies of Communication and Assimilation*

The shape of the utterances produced in the second language may be influenced by additional factors, not related to interference or to aspects of generalization and analogy. Under communication strategies we may include errors that derive from the fact that heavy communication demands may be made on the second language, forcing the learner to mold whatever he has assimilated of the second language into a means of saying what he wants to say, or of getting done what he wants to get done. The learner may simplify the syntax of the language in an effort to make the language into an instrument of his own intentions. Errors deriving from such efforts may be attributed to strategies of communication. Errors attributable to the learner's attempts to reduce the learning burden of what he has to assimilate may be closely related, and they may be referred to as strategies of assimilation.

Perhaps the clearest examples of alterations in language structure as a result of strategies of assimilation and communication are to be found in pidgin languages—languages used by people whose mother tongues are different, in order to facilitate communication between them. In the process of becoming a pidgin a language often loses some of its vocabulary, or is simplified in its phonology or grammar. Simplification is one way in which speakers of different languages can make a new language easier to learn and use (see Samarin, 1962).

We frequently find instances of a similar process in a normal second language setting. The communicative demands made on the second language may far outpace the speaker's actual competence in the second language, thus the speaker may have to create the means of expressing relations for which the language course has not prepared him. The school English course, for example, may begin with the present tense, the present continuous, and following concepts of linguistic grading or sequencing, delay the introduction of other tenses until the present and present continuous have been mastered. Supposing however, that the English program is that of an English-medium school in a multilingual context, where English provides the only lingua franca among Chinese-, Malay-, and Tamil-speaking children. The children in their use of English as a lingua franca outside of the classroom cannot wait until the past and "future" tenses have been taught before they will begin talking about past and planned events. They will have to establish their own way of dealing with past and planned events, and in so doing there will be considerable simplification of syntax, and extension of the uses of known forms into other areas. This may produce what has been called "dormitory English" and "playground English," which can function as an entirely efficient form of communication: *You are not knowing what Boonlat is do. He is open stand-pipe . . . water is not coming, so he go ask . . .* (example from a working paper by H. V. George).

This may seem an extreme example, but in any situation where the second language actually has to be used outside the classroom in real situations, inevitably the learner finds himself having to cope with circumstances that the school syllabus has not covered or for which he may not have the linguistic resources available. Looking at such language samples, we are often not able to say whether a particular error is attributable to a strategy of communication, or to a strategy of assimilation, that is, an identifiable approach by the learner to the material being learned.

My own acquisition of French in Quebec has provided me with many examples of the effects of communication and assimilation strategies, since on arrival in Quebec extensive demands were immediately made on whatever I had been able to pick up of the language. As an example of assimilation strategy, I found the form *je vais* (I'm going to) easier to learn than the future tense in French, and I quickly developed the means of expressing futurity or intention with the use of this construction. This however led me to use the *going to* form in situations where the future tense was appropriate, and now I frequently have to correct a tendency to use the *going to* form in sentences like *Je vais vous téléphoner ce soir* (I'm going to telephone you tonight) when what is really intended is *Je vous téléphonerai ce soir* (I'll telephone you tonight).

As an example of a communication strategy my acquisition of the conditional passé tense in French is illuminating. A language need that soon presented itself was the need to express intentions in the past that I was unable to fulfill. Since I did not acquire the grammatical means to do this until fairly late, I had to find alternative ways of expressing the same content. This I did by lexical means, through the use of a longer construction. Thus instead of saying, "I would have liked to have seen the film last night"—*J'aurais voulu voir le film hier soir*—I would say, "I had the intention of seeing the film last night, but . . . "—*J'avais l'intention de voir le film hier soir, mais . . .*

Similar strategies may account for the frequent misuse of the present tense as a narrative form, since the present tense is usually introduced first in language courses and the additional learning burden involved in acquiring the past tense can be avoided if the past is simply expressed lexically. A word like *yesterday* will thus suffice to locate the time setting and the speaker will continue in the present. *Yesterday we go for a drive and we stop near the beach and we . . .* Thus the speaker is able to expand the functional capacities of his knowledge of the second language, while keeping to known or sure ground.

The selection and gradation of items in a language course should therefore take account not merely of linguistic factors, such as the frequency or complexity of items to be introduced, but also the demands that will be made on the language and how the learner will adapt what he is given to his particular needs.

9.0 *Errors and the Teacher*

Teachers, as Pit Corder remarks, are more concerned with how to deal with errors than with what causes them, and in this there have been several schools of thought. "One is that if we were to achieve a perfect teaching method the errors would never be committed in the first place, and that therefore the occurrence of errors is merely a sign of the present inadequacy of our teaching techniques" (Corder, 1967). This attitude is illustrated in the introduction to a recent elementary English course. "One of the teacher's aims should be to prevent mistakes from occurring. In the early stages while the pupils are wholly dependent on the teacher for what they learn, it should be possible to achieve this aim" (Lee, 1970).

It is difficult to reconcile this approach with what we know or can observe about language learning. Children do not themselves acquire language by correctly imitating sentences they hear. "A child learns his language by interacting with it, by actively coping with and manipulating his environment. He does this on the basis of unsystematic, usually unplanned language input on the part of his parents" (Moores, 1970). Does this lead to an essential casualness on the part of the teacher towards the nature of the sentences his students produce? After all, current views of language learning emphasize that language cannot be taught, but must be learned by the child. Attempts to teach language by direct imposition of an adult grammatical model seem psycholinguistically inconsistent.

However, in assessing the teacher's role in second language teaching we are faced with the fact that although the child learning his mother tongue begins by producing sentences which do not duplicate adult sentences, gradually building towards an adult grammar, in second language learning what is usually the end point in the learning process is an Interlanguage, that is, a form differing from the target language characterized by interference both internal and external to the language. What we would have to postulate then is the encouragement of those types of sentences that indicate language development, and the minimization of opportunities for fossilization, for the establishment of permanent deficiencies in the learner's competence. In the present state of our knowledge about second language acquisition this is not a realizable goal, since we have so little information about which types of errors in second language learning are positive and which are negative. A form like *What he is doing?* may represent transitional competence in first language acquisition, but fossilization in the second language learner's speech. In the present state of our knowledge, we need to be careful not to be overoptimistic about the relevance to second language teaching of studies of first language acquisition.

At the same time, all language teaching techniques can be seen to produce transfer-of-training effects, where the general effects of memory on the material taught are apparent in reconstruction and retroactive inhibition as well as generalization and analogy. It is possible to try to arrange teaching materials to minimize the unwanted effects of such factors, but we have no way of knowing whether this is ultimately of any advantage to the learner. Questions, for example, invariably influence in unintended ways the form of the sentence the student uses in his answer. *What was the woman saying?* used to elicit sentences about a film will tend to elicit *The woman saying she will. . . . Ask her how long it takes* will produce *How long it takes?* and so on. Or if we introduce a text for practicing comparative constructions including *is as big as, is bigger than*, some of the students will produce *is as bigger as, is as big than*. Such effects might be minimized by separating the forms that interfere with each other and teaching them at different times, but we cannot say very much about what the results of particular instructional approaches will be on the final competence of the learner. It may make no difference at all, since there is no evidence that the linguistic and instructional variables—the points we select to teach and the order and manner in which we teach them—are the same as the psychological variables, the actual nature of the process by which the language items become part of the speaker's competence.

Despite the inadequacies of our present knowledge about the relevance of particular approaches to language instruction, there are excellent social motivations for teachers' drawing their learners' attention to examples of fossilization, to those errors that seem to have become a permanent rather than a transitional feature of their speech. In looking at the social justification for the correction of certain errors we can keep in mind, however, that linguistically we may simply be trying to modify our learner's performance rules. Even if his competence is represented in sentences like *Yesterday I go down town*, conscious attention to the way he speaks may assist him to modify his performance so that he produces *Yesterday I went down town*. If grammmatically deviant speech still serves to communicate the speaker's intentions, why should we pay further attention to it?

Simply because speech is linked to attitudes and social structure. Deviancy from grammatical or phonological norms of a speech community elicits evaluational reactions that may classify a person unfavorably. In sociolinguistic terms " . . . our speech, by offering a rich variety of social and ethnic correlates, each of which has attitudinal correlates in our own and our listener's behavior is one means by which we remind ourselves and others of social and ethnic boundaries, and is thus a part of the process of social maintenance (or change)" (Williams, 1970). Psychologists have investigated the way listeners will provide a range of reliable cultural, social class, and personality associations upon hearing speech samples. These are usually measured by playing recordings of speakers, and having them rated on a series of characteristics, such as intelligence, character, good looks, and so on. I propose that the adult second language learner's deviation from grammatical norms elicits evaluational reactions that can be measured in similar ways. My evidence is largely anecdotal. Here is an extract from a recent UNESCO report. "Individuals who learn new languages later in life, especially after the age of 15 or so, characteristically have more difficulty with new structures than with new vocabulary, and the difficulty seems to increase with age. It is not uncommon to characterize such people as 'having a foreign accent' or 'speaking brokenly,' even though their vocabulary and general fluency may be quite satisfactory in the acquired language. Although they have little difficulty in being understood for practical purposes, they are apt to be considered as perpetual foreigners or outsiders" (Noss, 1967).

My observations of native speakers' reactions to grammatical deviancy suggest that not all instances of deviancy, not all errors, are evaluated in the same way. We don't react to *I'm going in Paris next week* in the same way as we react to *I is going to Paris next week* or to *He come from India.* Omission of a third person *-s* or a plural seems to grate rather violently, whereas a misplaced preposition may not affect us so much. Deviancy in article usage may elicit a "baby-talk" evaluation. You may have noticed this in your own relations with nonnative speakers of English. One almost automatically corrects certain types of mistakes while we let others pass without too much thought.

Native speakers' reactions to systematic variation in grammatical or other features could be measured using the psychologists' techniques for measuring reactions to different dialects. This would demand systematically varying the nature of deviancy in oral or written texts and having native speakers assess the personality traits of the speakers.

Here is an example of a passage in which article usage is deviant:

I remember war period very clearly. I remember big bomb which exploded near house I was living in in 1940. First wall began to crack and window broke and I hurried out of house just before chimney fell down. I saw that big tree in front of house was broken.

Here is the same text with article usage restored but past tense omitted:

I remember the war period very clearly. I remember a big bomb which explode near the house I live in in 1940. First the wall begin to crack and the window break and I hurry out of the house just before the chimney fall down. I see that a big tree in front of the house is broken.

Information on the reaction of native speakers to particular aspects of grammatical deviancy would thus enable us to say which examples of fossilization the second language teacher should pay most attention to.

Conclusions

To draw together some of the points I have touched upon here, I have first of all tried to suggest why people who speak second languages may not speak or write them with native-speaker-like fluency. I have suggested that deficiencies in their knowledge may be the results of interference, the use of aspects of another language at a variety of levels; of strategies of learning such as overgeneralization and analogy by means of which the learner tests out his hypotheses about the structure of the language; of strategies of assimilation, in which the learner makes his learning task casier; and of strategies of communication, whereby the learner adapts what he knows into an efficient communication model, producing an optimal utility grammar from what he knows of the language.

At the same time we need to distinguish between performance and competence errors. The former are occasional and haphazard and are related to such factors as fatigue, memory limitations, and so on. The latter are systematic and may represent either a transitional stage in the development of a grammatical rule or the final stage of the speaker's knowledge. While our knowledge about second language learning is still largely speculative, excluding the possibility of prescribing recipes for teachers, I hope that this account of errors and learning strategies has at least suggested some of the reasons for what we hear from our students of second languages.

This is a revised version of a paper which appeared in *Language Sciences*, 17 (1971). It is reprinted here by permission of the author and publishers.

REFERENCES
Aguas, E. F. "English Composition Errors of Tagalog Speakers and Implications for Analytical Theory." Unpublished doctoral dissertation. University of California, Los Angeles, 1964.

Anstey, F. *A Bayard from Bengal*. London: Methuen, 1902.

Bellugi, U. "Linguistic Mechanisms Underlying Child Speech."(ed.), E. M. Zale. *Proceedings of the Conference on Language and Language Behavior*, pp. 36-50. New York: Appleton-Century-Crofts, 1968.

Corder, S. P. "The Significance of Learners' Errors." *IRAL*, 5 (1967), 161-169.

Dušková, L. "On Sources of Errors in Foreign Langauge Learning." *IRAL*, 7 (1969), 11-36

Falk, J. "Nominalizations in Spanish." *Studies in Linguistics and Language Learning V.* Seattle: University of Washington Press, 1968.

Ferguson, C. "Diglossia." *Word* 15 (1959), 325-40.

French, F. G. *Common Errors in English*. London: Oxford University Press, 1949.

George, H. V. "Teaching Simple Past and Past Perfect." *Bulletin of the Central Institute of English* (Hyderabad, India), 2 (1962), 18-31.

Jakobovits, L. A. *Foreign Language Learning*. Rowley, Mass.: Newbury House.

Jones, R. *System in Child Language*. Aberystwyth: University of Wales Press, 1970.

Kaplan, R. "Contrastive Rhetoric and the Teaching of Composition." *TESOL Quarterly*, 1.4 (1967), 10-16.

Kinzel, P. *Lexical and Grammatical Interference in the Speech of a Bilingual Child*. Seattle: University of Washington, 1964.

Lado, R. *Linguistics Across Cultures*. Ann Arbor: University of Michigan Press, 1957.

Lee, W. R. *The Dolphin English Course; Teacher's Companion*. London: Oxford University Press, 1970.

Leopold, W. F. *Speech Development of a Bilingual Child*. 4 vols. Evanston: Northwestern University Press, 1939-1949.

Macmillan, M. "Aspects of Bilingualism in University Education in Sudan." (ed.), T. Gorman. *Language and Education in East Africa*. Nairobi: Oxford University Press, 1970.

Moores, D. F. "Psycholinguistics and Deafness."*American Annals of the Deaf*, 39 (January, 1970).

Noss, R. *Higher Education and Development in South East Asia*. Paris: UNESCO, 1967.

Richards, J. C. "A Non-Contrastive Approach to Error Analysis." *English Language Teaching*, 25 (1971), 204-219. (This volume, pp. 96-113.)

Samarin, W. J. "Lingua Francas, with Special Reference to Africa." (ed.), F. Rice, *Study of the Role of Second Languages in Asia, Africa, and Latin America*, pp. 54-64. Washington: Center for Applied Linguistics, 1962.

Selinker, L. "The Psychologically-relevant Data of Second Language Learning." Paper read at the Second International Congress of Applied Linguistics, Cambridge, England, 1969a. In P. Pimsleur and T. Quinn (eds.) *The Psychology of Second Language Learning*. Cambridge University Press, 1972, 35-44.

———. "Language Transfer." *General Linguistics*, 9.2 (1969b), 67-92.

Slobin, D. "Suggested Universals in the Ontogenesis of Grammar." Working Paper 32, Language Behavior Research Laboratory, University of California, Berkeley, 1970.

Wardhaugh, R. "The Contrastive Analysis Hypothesis." *TESOL Quarterly*, 4.2 (1970), 123-30.

Williams, F. "Language Attitude and Social Change." (ed. id.), *Language and Poverty*, Chicago: Markham, 1970.

Wolfe, D. K. "Some Theoretical Aspects of Language Learning and Language Teaching." *Language Learning*, 17, 3-4 (1967), 181.

e.
INDUCED ERRORS

NANCY STENSON

1.0 *Introduction*

In this paper, I would like to describe some types of student errors in a language classroom that result more from the classroom situation than from either the student's incomplete competence in English grammar or first language interference. Students are easily led into making errors in the course of classroom participation by the structure of the situation; these are errors which it is doubtful they would produce in spontaneous speech. Such induced errors tell us little about the level of the student's language competence but are worthy of study in that they are easy to overlook, may easily cause inaccurate assessment of the student's ability, and, if ignored, may reinforce misunderstanding and form the basis for later problems. Any analysis of student errors must also take such mistakes into account as phenomena separate from errors of spontaneous speech.

The data from which my examples are drawn was gathered in Tunis, Tunisia, during the summer of 1971 from observation of adult English classes at the Institut Bourguiba des Langues Vivantes, and from high school students during practice teaching sessions of the 1971 Peace Corps TEFL training program in Mahdia, Tunisia. Most of the students were in intermediate or advanced classes.

2.0 *Vocabulary*

A teacher may inadvertently mislead students by the way he defines a lexical item, or by the order in which he presents material. For example, given *worship* as a general word for *pray*, the students immediately attached to the new word the same preposition that they knew to be required with the familiar one, and began speaking of "worshipping to God". Habits which may develop from such analogies between two related items seem especially difficult to break; several students made this mistake in succession, even after the teacher had corrected the first of them.

The problems of both word definition and order of presentation were brought into focus when students were confronted for the first time with a single lexical item consisting of a verb + particle. They

were given the definition of *point out* through example sentences
with appropriate gestures, and then asked to use it in sentences.
Those students who did not merely paraphrase the teacher's
examples were all clearly treating the construction as two separate
lexical items, *point,* which they already knew, and the preposition
out. Thus, the new lexical item came out sounding to them like just
another way to say *point to* or *point at.* One student with a little
more imagination offered "When I see a ship in the sea, I point out",
which the teacher corrected to ". . . I point it out to my friends."
This is probably not what the student meant at all. The chances are
at least equally good that he was using *out* as a directional: "I point
out (to sea, to the ship, etc.). . ." That he intended *out* in his
sentence to indicate direction is plausible, since all students were
having a great deal of trouble with *point out,* and since omission of a
direct object pronoun where one is required was rare, if not unheard
of, at least among these students. If this were the case, the teacher's
insertion of the pronoun *it* is no help at all to the student. It doesn't
help him learn the real meaning of *point out,* which both the teacher
and he assume he knows, and if he's a very attentive student, given to
quick generalizations, he might even be led, by a correction like this,
to start inserting *it* incorrectly with other directionals. Treating verb
+ particle forms as a unit at some point would at least give a tool for
correcting individual lexical items.

Immediately after *point out,* and without fully understanding it,
the students were given *notice* and asked to use it in sentences. This
led to the sentence "The barometer noticed that it wouldn't be
fine." This student appears to have confused the two new vocabulary
items and, since one word bears a causative relation to the other, this
serves to reinforce the confusion. The student might not make a
mistake like this in a normal conversation—he would be more
inclined to use a word he's sure of, like *show,* if he ever needed to
talk about barometer readings—but once he has misused a word or
(worse) a pair of words, even under drill conditions, he will probably,
if not set straight, remain confused and make additional errors. This
is not to suggest that a teacher should necessarily avoid teaching
related words together. Indeed, such a device can be a very useful
teaching technique, and whether to use it or not must depend on the
situation and the class. However, a teacher who is attuned to such
relationships between words (not always evident on the surface of
things) can do much to avoid difficulties or clear them up once they
present themselves.

A final type of induced vocabulary error came from students being forced to demonstrate a distinction that they were vaguely aware of, but unable to explain adequately. For example, asked to demonstrate the difference between *should* and *must,* a student said: "We should have worked in order to buy clothes, but we must have worked in order to eat." This class knew that *must* was in some way stronger than *should,* but were apparently not entirely clear on just how—in general, they steered clear of *should* and used *must* everywhere. The student who had to demonstrate the difference did indeed make a distinction of degree, but in so doing, he transferred the force of necessity from the end to the means.

A similar error arose when a student attempted to characterize the difference between *at* and *into*: "We look at the moon, but Armstrong looked into the moon." The distinction had been demonstrated solely by examples and pantomime ("Now I'm looking at the bag; now I'm looking *into* the bag" [moving closer to the bag to indicate peering into it]) and this student probably got the idea that the distinction was one of thoroughness or closeness rather than of surface versus interior. Just saying "no" to a student with such a misconception teaches him nothing, yet a teacher unaware of what is going on can do little else.

Situations like these can tell us a lot we wouldn't otherwise learn about what a student knows and doesn't know. It is impossible to measure his competence with structures and vocabulary he never uses. Since errors are our only way of determining what aspects of language the student has not yet acquired, one could easily be led to assume (without the help of induced errors) that non-appearance of a certain structure rather than deviant appearance indicates acquisition of that structure. In many cases nothing could be farther from the truth. The difference between systematic errors which reflect possible rule differences, interference, etc., and those errors arising from gaps in student grammar should be obvious. The latter constructions are extremely difficult to get at, since they are rarely (and never systematically) reflected in the student's speech. Thus a tremendous number of differences between a student's competence and that of a native speaker may go unobserved or unexplained because there is no data to work from. Here, then, is an area where the importance of induced errors as distinguished from spontaneous errors is apparent. The former provide otherwise unobtainable information about student competence. Two points follow from this: first, that vocabulary misuse may reflect non-acquisition of certain structural elements in the language rather than misunderstanding of a lexical definition; second, errors that might be *describable* in terms of differences in rule formulation between student and native grammar will not necessarily be *explained* in this way. The following section further illustrates this.

3.0 *Syntax*

Grammatical errors that wouldn't ordinarily occur may also be induced through misunderstanding of meaning or usage, or, occasionally, through faulty explanation. Students in one advanced class were asked if they knew the meaning of *any,* and, when all said yes, to give some examples, with the following result: "In this class there are any students who speak German (=not any, no students)", "In a private garden anyone can enter (=no one)" and "Anybody has to work." Apparently these students were once told something to the effect that *any* is used in negatives, or has negative connotations, and they interpreted that to mean that it was itself a negative word, like *never* or *nothing.* Thus, in the first two sentences above, the students left the negative marker off the verb as redundant, producing, in the first case, a deviant sentence, and in the second a polarity switch. The third sentence seems to involve a confusion between *any* and *every* (cf. " $\begin{Bmatrix} \text{Everybody} \\ \text{Anybody} \end{Bmatrix}$ may leave now.").

That these are situation-induced errors is suggested by the fact that students, even at advanced levels, tend not to use *any* and other words involving feature shifts at all, though they would probably understand them if encountered in someone else's speech. In fact, "I don't have some NP" is a common type of student error; on the other hand, I found no other cases of misuse of negative polarity words, probably because such words are among the last things learned, and hence almost never used, even at advanced levels.

One teacher defined *as if* as more or less synonymous with *like* and then asked students to transform sentences with *like* into sentences with *as if* (e.g., "He climbs like a monkey" into "He climbs as if he were a monkey."). But one student, given the sentence "She cries like a baby" responded with "She cries as if the baby cries" which would be fine if *like* were really just a synonym for *as if.* In fact, however, there is a structural change involved in this exercise as well. The sentence the student was asked to transform is ambiguous; it could be paraphrased in either of the following ways:

Her crying is like that of a baby. (she cries like a baby cries)

In that she cries, she is just like a baby. (she cries like she is a baby)

It is only in the second of these two readings that *as if* can be used. The student has inserted *as if* in the first sentence with incorrect results. The average native speaker of English would not normally be conscious of the above ambiguity until an incorrect sentence appeared such as the one this student produced. It is crucial, however, that the teacher be aware of such potential ambiguities and avoid inadequate explanations like the one given in this case. A thorough understanding of the syntax of sentences with *like* in them is the only way to make clear to the student when *as if* can be substituted for *like* and when it cannot.

A final danger lies in overreliance on grammatical terminology without sufficient attention to function in the sentence. Thus, after several examples involving *absolutely impossible*, students asked to use the adjective form of *absolutely* produced: "It's absolute impossible to do." These students had fairly thorough familiarity with grammatical terminology and usage, so it may have been sheer laziness that produced this sentence. In any case, such an error is simple enough to correct, especially where the students are acquainted with the terms. But it is not the sort of mistake they usually made spontaneously and can thus be attributed to careless reliance on terminology at the expense of the usage it represents, rather than to real confusion over form and function. As such, it is probably not worth spending much time on, and should be recognized for what it is.

4.0 *Drills*

It is easy to fall into the pattern of a structural drill and forget that the sentences being produced have semantic content; in reducing textbook exercises to rote mechanical repetition, students produce some bizarre semantic violations that would be unlikely to appear in real speech. An intermediate level drill gave students the choice of several phrases as possible responses to a yes-no question:

No, but I $\begin{cases} \text{hope to} \\ \text{ought to} \\ \text{must} \\ \text{expect to} \\ \text{have to} \\ \text{etc.} \end{cases}$

Thus, "Do you want to study? No, but I have to." Some of the students responded with no apparent regard for any semantic relationship between the question and their choice of response: "Are you going to the movies? No, but I hope to"; "Do you want to study tonight? No, but I hope to"; "Does she understand French? No, but she must."[1] It may have been mere lack of attention that caused such errors (only the students can know), but even those students who were listening in seemed to notice nothing peculiar in them. From the responses students were making, it appeared that they didn't really understand the exercise or the meaning of the tag they were being asked to put on their answers. Again, this sort of thing would not occur in normal speech, but probably only because they have not in fact learned the construction and hence wouldn't use it spontaneously. Such exercises need to be carefully monitored to prevent students from making a mistake set up for them by a possible wrong choice, and above all to avoid reinforcing misconceptions. Where this is not done, students are likely either to not understand or to mislearn. The first would render the drill meaningless; the second would make it detrimental.

Another sort of exercise has the opposite effect of rigidly dictating the students' responses where there are other valid possibilities. Thus, a *not*-insertion drill was preceded by the following instructions:

If the negative can be contracted with an auxiliary do so. Otherwise, put *not* before the infinitive.

as in: "John can write ⟶ John can't write"; "John prefers to write ⟶ John prefers not to write." In the first example above, it is the modal *can* which is being negated, not the verb *write*, whereas in the second case negation is associated with *write* rather than the preceding *prefer*. As if it weren't enough that students had two different structures to work with in the same drill, the majority of sentences of the second type involved matrix verbs of the type *expect*, where there are two possibilities for negative placement, with a corresponding difference in scope and meaning. Moreover, the "correct" response was often the less common of the two possibilities. Students were expected to say:

$$\text{John} \begin{Bmatrix} \text{expects} \\ \text{wants} \\ \text{etc.} \end{Bmatrix} \text{not to go.}$$

with the predictable result that they were torn between what they were instructed to say and what they had so often heard and tried to imitate: "John doesn't expect to go." In addition, they had to cope with input sentences like "He will continue to answer" where both contraction-after-modal or *not*-before-infinitive are possible, and "He needs to study" with its variety of possibilities for negation:

He $\begin{cases} \text{doesn't need to} \\ \text{needs not to} \\ \text{need not (needn't)} \end{cases}$ study"

the latter in its uncontracted form being the one taught, for no discernible reason and with no explanation.[2]

A third potential source of trouble in exercises can be found in those drills which involve the joining of two simple sentences in which grammatical transformations have applied which would not apply in the complex sentence. Thus, for example, students were asked to embed one of two sentences in the other by using one of the conjunctions *unless, because, if, although, whenever, whether or not,* as in the following:

The air conditioner isn't working. The students enjoy the class.

⟶ The students enjoy the class $\begin{cases} \text{unless} \\ \text{although} \\ \text{etc.} \end{cases}$ the air conditioner isn't working.

Taking an imperative sentence as part of his input, one student produced the following: "I can't buy any new shoes unless lend me some money" (from "Lend me some money. I can't buy any new shoes."). That is, he joined the surface strings, as they were given to him, and of course imperatives can't occur in the resulting environment.

What is interesting is not so much this mistake (which is not surprising and is easy to correct) as the fact that in other cases where students were thus given an opportunity to make a mistake from the input to their drill, they did not. One pair of sentences given in the same exercise as that just discussed was this: "Paul is too busy. He takes a nap every afternoon." Joining these with *unless,* one would expect "*He takes a nap every afternoon unless Paul is too busy" which is a violation of the rules of pronoun reference. In fact, however, this did not occur. Students changed the sentence to avoid this deviance: "He takes a nap every afternoon unless he is too busy" or "Paul takes a nap every afternoon unless he is too busy," and in other cases, students were able to form various complex sentences involving pronominalization, always keeping the pronoun-antecedent relations straight.

Clues to the question of which possible errors students avoid despite inducements to make them may lie in the notion of linguistic universals. The notion of command relationships and the constraints on pronominalization associated with them have been proposed as universal to all languages. See Langacker (1969) for a discussion of the notion of command. Bever (1970) has formulated this as a perceptual constraint to the effect that one element cannot stand for another unless a connection has already been established or it is apparent (as through a marker of subordination) that such a connection is about to be established. In either case, it would not be surprising for a student to avoid violating a universal constraint. Imperative formation, on the other hand, differs from language to language (although some form of imperative is universal). Thus, Arabic does not distinguish imperative sentences from declaratives by subject deletion as does English. It would be interesting to examine whether students whose native language does form imperatives by subject deletion would make the same mistake. This is an area where theoretical linguistics and teaching can perhaps be mutually useful, the research on universals (syntactic or cognitive) providing a possible explanation for the occurrence and non-occurrence of certain errors, and the classroom providing a place to test hypotheses about universals.

5.0 *Unexpected Errors*

5.1 *Common errors.* There were other types of errors that students insisted on making, despite strong inducements to avoid them, for example, students at all levels often substituted *his* for *her* and *her* for *their*, both in free speech and in reading, when the correct form was right in front of them. They had particular trouble with the final *s* of the plural (noun) and third person singular (verb) and often left it out, even when reading, as in "How's the work these day, Jack?" (from a reading exercise). An example of just how difficult the *-s* ending is can be seen in the following: in a simple substitution drill where students were to change the subject of a sentence as indicated by the teacher and change the form of the verb where necessary, the following exchange took place:

Student$_1$:	He is often here.
Teacher:	The students
Student$_2$:	The student is often here.
Teacher:	Studentsssss
Student$_2$:	They are often here.
Teacher:	Say studentsssss
Student$_2$:	The student are often here.

This student clearly knew, at least by the end of the exchange, that a plural was involved, and knew how to form the plural for the verb, but try as he would the teacher could not get her to pronounce the plural morpheme -s on the noun.

Tense was another frequent problem, and particularly certain sequence of tense rules. Thus, there were mistakes such as "[In the old days, parents arranged weddings and] the boy didn't know the girl he is going to marry" or "After a long travel, I returned to my house and see a lot of dust." The following sentence "He acts as if he knows Habib Bourguiba" was given in response to the exercise changing *like* to *as if* (contrary to fact). The students had been told repeatedly that *as if* requires a past verb for a counterfactual meaning, and in this case the input sentence given by the teacher already had the correct verb form in it, ("He acts as if he knew H.B."), so that there was no change or choice that the student needed to make to produce the expected "He acts as if he knew Habib Bourguiba". Yet he changed the tense, and thus the meaning of the sentence. In cases like this, apparently the student's difficulty with the form overcame all the positive clues he was given.

In general, students had far less trouble with the past tense in simple sentences, although errors such as "I forget to say to you that . . . " and "Do they have lunch yesterday" did occur on a random basis, even among advanced students.

5.2 *Atypical errors.* Not all errors made in these circumstances are typical in other contexts, however. A common instance of a situation where all the right information is available is the pattern drill, where students have just one transformation to perform, leaving the rest of the sentence intact. One of the purposes of this sort of drill is precisely to militate against extraneous, irrelevant errors, and as has been discussed above, students tend to take this sort of instruction quite literally, and where an exercise is not carefully written, may in fact produce a deviant sentence by choosing the wrong lexical item to insert or by failing to make some secondary change which goes along with the transformation being drilled. But where there is truly only one change to be made, one expects the student to leave the rest of the sentence alone (and herein lies the ease in ignoring its meaning altogether). It is therefore surprising to find a student reordering other elements in a sentence in the course of a drill, even where word order may be troublesome elsewhere in his speech. In a passive formation drill, a student given "We always keep our knives in this drawer" produced the following: "Our knives are kept in this draw always." While some students have difficulty with the order of constituents in English, adverb placement, at least with simple tenses, is not generally a troublemaker. The fact that the simple present is changed to an Auxiliary + participle construction may be the source of trouble, but what one would expect, on the basis of similar spontaneously made errors, would be something like "Our knives are kept always in this drawer." I know of no precedent or explanation for reordering the adverb with respect to the prepositional phrase in the course of the drill.

In a dialogue that was being learned by repetition and memorization, the following sentences were produced: "Ours is much newer model," and "His must be a one of the newest models." In a similar case, students were forming sentences on the pattern "Verb+ing is fun," "X-ing is hard work"; one student said "Walking is a good exercise." The first of these sentences represents one of the most common mistakes made by Tunisian students—omission of the article. In the next two cases, however, an article has been inserted, something far rarer in free conversation. These may be cases of overcorrection; a grammatical explanation could no doubt also be found. It is peculiar, however, that this occurs here, where the model for the correct sentence without the article is available to the student and is the more natural one for him in any case.

The above error types represent an entirely different situation from those described in earlier sections. The sentences discussed in 5.1 are examples of patterns that also occur frequently in spontaneous speech, and which are so strongly a part of the student's grammar that they are preferred even where the correct form is obvious. The examples in this section, on the other hand, represent a peculiar subset of induced errors. Like induced errors, the cases described above do not occur in normal speech, but here the situation in the classroom is set up not for them *to be made*, but for them *NOT to be made*. Yet they occur despite everything and are, apparently, thoroughly internalized into the student's grammar. Thus they should perhaps not be considered errors in the same sense as those discussed in the bulk of this paper, but rather as Corder (1971) suggests, manifestations of rule differences between the student's idiosyncratic dialect and the native dialect he is learning.

6.0 *The Problem of Meaning*

It is often unclear what a student means to say when he produces an ungrammatical sentence, particularly when it has no context, as in answer to a teacher's request to "give me a sentence using X." One student, when asked to give a sentence using *as if* (which had just been defined as a synonym of *like* with the second clause in the past for negative implication), said "I am glad as if I had slept." It is not at all clear what is wrong with this sentence because the meaning that the student had in mind is obscure (does he mean: glad because I slept, glad that I slept, would be glad if I'd slept, would like to have slept, didn't sleep but feel as if I had?). Since the teacher didn't ask the student to explain, he could not do more than just say "you can't say that in English," and we can do no more than mention it as an unclear example.

In a lesson on gerunds, students were questioned in such a way that they produced sentences with gerundive subjects:

Teacher: What do you do on the weekend?
Student$_1$: I go swimming.
Teacher: Is it fun?
Student$_1$: Yes.
Teacher: What's fun?
Student$_2$: Swimming is fun.

One such sequence went as follows:

Teacher: What does your father do?
Student$_1$: He's director of a bank.
Teacher: Is it hard work?
Student$_1$: Yes.
Teacher: What's hard work?
Student$_2$: Hard work is the director of a bank.

This is an example of the error type discussed in section 5.2 above, where the student ignores a drill situation which sets him up for the correct response, and produces a deviant sentence as a result. The clue to what might be happening in these cases must be sought in the student's intended meaning. One could hypothesize several different possibilities for this sentence, taken in isolation. Notice, for example, that the above response is identical in form to a different type of WH-question-answer pair:

Q: What is an apple?
A: An apple is a fruit.

where the questioned noun phrase subject is defined by qualification in the predicate. That is, in one case, the predicate provides the new information, and in the other, the subject does. The question here is whether the student really has confused the two: did he misunderstand the question or simply now know how to form the answer? It seems unlikely in a case where several correct sentences on the same pattern had already been elicited that he would suddenly do a semantic reverse like this. In fact, we have already seen that evidence seems to indicate that the opposite is more often the case. That is, if in the middle of a series of sentence pairs of the pattern "What is fun? Swimming is fun," the teacher said "What is an apple?", a student with poor command of wh-questions might respond, in the same pattern, with "Fruit is an apple." The pattern is not broken, even when it should be. It is more likely in this instance that the student understood the question and had the correct answer in mind. It was only coincidental that, in garbling the grammar of his answer, he stumbled upon *another* English syntactic pattern. The question then remains, why did he make a mistake, and what should the teacher do about it? Is it enough simply to give the right answer, with no explanation of why the sentence was wrong? Or should the teacher take the time to find out exactly what the student meant, and show him why he didn't succeed in expressing it? If his problem is something as simple as not knowing what to do with the object of the gerund, merely hearing the correct sentence might be enough. But the teacher must know his student well to be sure the problem isn't deeper, especially where the student's sentence falls so close to another correct English pattern *and* where the drill situation would lead one to expect the right answer. Even if he didn't have the definition-type sentence in mind, he might still notice the resemblance later and get confused. Alternatively, the student may, as has been suggested by Corder (1967), simply be testing a hypothesis about the new language by the sentence he has produced and will accept the correction. The only way to tell in such cases is by studying the persistence of errors over time. The teacher, who sees his students regularly over a period of time, has access to the evidence necessary for an accurate determination, and can thus provide a valuable service to the researcher doing error analysis.

It may not even be clear in every case whether a sentence a student produces is deviant or not. For example, in a class asked to make up sentences using *should,* one student said, "They should need another book." If *should* is taken to mean expectation on the part of the speaker, this sentence is fine ("They should need another book by next week, because they're on the last chapter of this one already"). But it is unlikely that this is what the student meant, since this class was just learning modals for the first time, and *should,* even in its more common sense of *ought to* was not an active part of their vocabulary. On the other hand, co-occurrence restrictions such as these are seldom violated in spontaneous speech, and it is unlikely that a sentence such as this would have been produced if the student had not been put on the spot. An analysis which does not take this into account overlooks an important principle which every teacher knows: the importance of context as an aid in deciphering student speech.

Of course, the time spent in trying to figure out what a student meant may not always be justifiable in the classroom. But it is important for the teacher to be aware of all the possibilities in order to make this decision. Correcting the wrong thing, or the right thing for the wrong reason, or not correcting enough, can easily make matters worse.

7.0 Summary and Conclusions

In the weak version of contrastive analysis, as in all forms of error analysis, the source of the error is an important issue (unlike the strong version of contrastive analysis, where the source is assumed). A great deal of evidence has come to light indicating that contrastive analysis is inadequate to explain the source of certain types of error. My research in Tunisia has reaffirmed this. But error analysis, as it is usually defined, also begs the question. Too many variables are involved to say that the idiosyncrasies of learner language are explainable solely in terms of either interference or target-language-internal rules, or even a combination of the two. In this paper, I have concentrated on errors which are related to the classroom situation itself. These fall into several categories. The first, and most obvious, are the errors which students wouldn't make in free speech, but which are elicited by the teacher's questions or by drills. These may be due to incomplete acquisition of the lexical item or grammatical structure involved, to analogy suggested by the order of presentation, or to a number of other possible causes, as yet unexplored.

I also touched briefly on some errors which one might expect to find within this framework, but which students manage to avoid. The relationship of potential errors which do not actually occur to putative linguistic universals such as co-reference restrictions, semantic restrictions, meaning conflicts, etc., is worth exploring. To this end, a thorough study of what errors are *not* made will be necessary. In addition, there are errors that recur despite a teaching situation designed to avoid them. These errors may provide evidence for the hypothesis-strategy approach to language learning suggested by Corder. If such is the case, it may turn out not to be worthwhile to force extensive drill of these issues when the learner isn't ready to absorb them.

The discussions above are intended to be highly tentative, as evidenced by the fact that no attempt is made to provide any solutions. It is first necessary to point out the *possible* sources of error, in order to increase awareness of the problems. Doubtless induced errors should be treated differently in the classroom (as well as in research) from those which actually reflect the student's developing competence, but it is not clear just how this is to be done.

Several issues are involved here. In preparing materials and writing drills, it is important to keep in mind that surface relationships could lead to misunderstanding on a deeper level, and that any inexplicit explanation may be open to misinterpretation by the student. The teacher must be on guard to monitor drills and explanations to be certain that they do not lead to false generalizations. In this way, many induced errors could be avoided or caught before they cause any real trouble. There is also the question of what to do about those errors which will crop up and persist despite all attempts to control them. It is here that the issue of ascertaining the student's meaning plays an important role. The clearer a teacher's understanding of the sources of student errors, the better he will be able to judge which ones are most worth concentrating on. Finally, an understanding of the effect on the student of miscorrection through misinterpretation of his intent is vital to adequate language teaching. No teacher would disagree that correcting the wrong thing could be disastrous; however, it is not always obvious especially to the inexperienced teacher, what is the right and what is the wrong thing. Only after this is determined, and only over an extended period of time, can the nature and extent of damage that such cases might cause be measured.

For the linguist studying second-language acquisition, the distinction between classroom-induced errors and spontaneous student errors is also valuable. It is crucial to bear this distinction in mind when attempting to account for student language, for to ignore it is to risk faulty analysis. It could cloud the issues to attribute to a developing grammar an error that the student wouldn't ordinarily make. It is of course quite possible to *describe* many, and perhaps all, of the errors discussed above solely in terms of rule deviance. For example, one could describe the confusion between *point out* and *notice* described in section 2.0 as simply a patient-agent confusion in the student's grammar, or the inability to distinguish between *should* and *must* by formally giving them a slightly different meaning from that of standard English. But such statements would be misleading if the description of student language is to have any reality in terms of the student's acquisition of the language, for these errors do not in fact represent any internalized part of his grammar, and do not therefore occur systematically in the same way that certain errors of tense usage or word order might occur. "Whenever a student of a second language creates an utterance in the second language, he reveals something about his competence (or his lack of competence)" (Wardhaugh, 1967). The errors discussed above suggest something about what the student does *not* know rather than about what he does know. We must not make the mistake of attributing them to a system where none exists. An approach to student language *description* which does not distinguish between spontaneous, systematic errors and those forced by the situation will do nothing to *explain* where the student is in the second language acquisition process, how he got there, or what the process is.

This article is published for the first time in this volume.

NOTES

This work was supported in part by Contract OEC-0-70-4986 from the U.S. Office of Education to the Language Research Foundation. I am endebted to many people who helped me in my research both here and in Tunisia. I would like especially to express my thanks to Mohammed Maamouri of the Institut Bourguiba des Langues Vivantes, Tunis, who arranged for me to attend English classes there, to DeWayne Coambs, Leslie and Lewis Tremaine, Mike Vale, and other Peace Corps staff members for access to their classrooms, and for helpful discussions of their own experiences at the beginning stages of my research, and to Bruce Fraser, Walt Olson, Patty Regan and John Schumann for their valuable comments on earliers versions of this paper.

1. This latter example is not necessarily an example of a semantic violation; in fact it may reflect a common spontaneous error type among students at this level: the substitution of *must* for *should*. Note that a response "No, but she should" would have þeen perfectly acceptable. This may well be what the student was saying. The same may be true of other examples I have used. This points up once again the extreme tentativeness of any claim about what the student actually meant to say.

2. This is a classic example of the deep/surface structure conflict: two sentences which have the same structure on the surface are quite different at a deeper, more abstract level. An awareness of current research in transformational linguistics can help the teacher find and avoid many such areas of difficulty.

REFERENCES

Banathy, Bela H., and Paul H. Madarasz (1969) "Contrastive Analysis and Error Analysis" *Journal of English as a Second Language*, IV:2, pp. 77-92.

Bever, Thomas G. (1970) "The Cognitive Basis for Linguistic Structures" in Hayes, John R. (ed.) *Cognition and the Development of Language*, New York & London: John Wiley & Sons, Inc.

Bowen, J. Donald (1967) "Contrastive Analysis and the Language Classroom" in Robinett, Betty Wallace (ed.) *On Teaching English to Speakers of Other Languages, Series III*, Papers read at the TESOL Conference, New York, March 17-19, 1966. Washington, D.C.: TESOL.

Burt, M. K. and Carol Kiparsky (1972) *The Gooficon*, Rowley, Mass.: Newbury House Publishers, Inc.

Buteau, Magdelhayne F. (1970) "Students' Errors and the Learning of French as a Second Language: A Pilot Study" *International Review of Applied Linguistics and Language Teaching (IRAL)* VIII:3, pp. 133-145.

Chomsky, Noam (1965) *Aspects of the Theory of Syntax*, Cambridge, Mass.: MIT Press.

——— (1966) "Linguistic Theory" in Robert G. Mead, Jr., (ed.) *Language Teaching: Broader Contexts*, Northeast Conference Reports, 1966.

Corder, S.P. (1967) "The Significance of Learners' Errors", *IRAL* V:4, pp. 161-169.

Corder, S.P. (1971) "Idiosyncratic Dialects and Error Analysis" *IRAL* IX:2, pp. 147-159.

Dušková, Libuse (1969) "On Sources of Errors in Foreign Language Learning" *IRAL* VII:1, pp. 11-36.

Jacobs, Roderick (1969) "Linguistic Universals and Their Relevance to TESOL" *TESOL Quarterly* III:2, pp. 117-122.

James, Carl (1969) "Deeper Contrastive Study" *IRAL* VII: 2.

Langacker, Ronald W. (1969) "Pronominalization and the Chain of Command" in D. Reibel and S. Schane (eds.) *Modern Studies in English*, Englewood Cliffs, N.J.: Prentice Hall.

Richards, Jack C. (1970) "A Non-Contrastive Approach to Error Analysis" ERIC, ED 037 721, paper presented at TESOL Convention, San Francisco, March 1970.

——— (1971) "Error Analysis and Second Language Strategies" *Language Sciences* No. 17, Bloomington, Indiana, pp. 12-22.

Rutherford, William E. (1968) "Deep Structure, Surface Sturcture, and Language Drill" *TESOL Quarterly* II:2, pp. 71-79.

Strevens, Peter (1969) "Two Ways of Looking at Error Analysis" ERIC, ED 037 714.

Wardhaugh, Ronald (1967) "Some Current Problems in Second Language Teaching" *Language Learning* XVII:1&2, pp. 21-26.

――― (1970) "The Contrastive Analysis Hypothesis" *TESOL Quarterly* IV:2, pp. 123-129.

f.
GLOBAL AND LOCAL MISTAKES

MARINA K. BURT & CAROL KIPARSKY

1.0 *Introduction*

We have found many English as a Second Language (ESL) classes where: (1) the motivation for teaching is to get the students to speak flawless English, (2) grammar topics are presented in order of difficulty from the point of view of English syntax, and (3) all mistakes are corrected with equal vigor.

In training, prospective teachers of English spend a large part of their time learning the rules of English grammar, and how to teach these rules to non-speakers of English. But the classroom situation demands more than just knowing all the rules and knowing what rules to teach. First, the rules alone don't help the teacher to anticipate the many kinds of mistakes he will hear. Since mistakes far outnumber correctly formed English sentences, it is useful for the teacher to have some idea of what kinds to expect so he will be prepared to handle them. Second, the teacher has no guide but his intuition to tell him which kinds of mistakes are most important to correct. If his goal is teaching his students to speak flawless, correct English, all mistakes seem about equally important, and so he naturally attempts to correct them all. As a consequence, many of the mistakes which are corrected are superficial, and some bad ones always seem to remain.

To help the teacher both in training and in the classroom, we have collected a number of mistakes actually made by foreign students from a variety of countries. These mistakes are both oral and written, in and out of class. In this paper we will attempt to find a principled basis for a hierarchy of errors which a teacher can use to determine what is most important to correct. The examples were taken from Peace Corps materials prepared by volunteers while teaching in the following countries: Ethiopia, Korea, Nigeria, Venezuela. We present mistakes from a variety of countries to reveal the areas in English grammar where difficulties often arise. The particular mistakes in some area of English may vary with the language background of the students, but syntactic areas in which trouble appears are quite general. In this paper, we consider only the syntax of English. Phonology and semantics are not considered.

One area of syntax which can cause trouble is the skeleton of the English sentence: the subject, verb, and object. There are two apparently simple facts about these major constituents and their role in declarative English sentences that cause some difficulty in learning English: (1) these constituents appear in a fixed order: subject-verb-object, (2) with transitive verbs, none of these constituents is optional. The mistakes that result from not learning these principles are misorderings leading to garbled grammatical relations in the first case, and ellipsis of major constituents in the second:

1) # The fish ate the child[1]

2) # Even though screamed and fought.

   # Too bad nobody rescued.

Most ESL books do not expose such problems. Discussion is often restricted to an announcement like "English word order is Subject-Verb-Object," which is not enough for certain students. If word order is a problem, it must be given high priority when determining what to correct in student speech.

Word order and non-optionality of major constituents are, in addition, a prerequisite for the discussion of many other topics, for they influence the comprehensibility of sentences in complex ways.

These are the sorts of considerations we have in mind when we speak of a "hierarchy of errors." In terms of comprehension, this hierarchy may be defined as follows:

> A is higher than B in the hierarchy if the correction of A contributes more to comprehensibility than the correction of B.

There is a systematic equivocation in our terminology. The items that are ranked in the hierarchy, called A and B above, are seen on the one hand as types of mistakes, and on the other hand as the part of the grammar (rules or other description) which is violated to produce such mistakes. Thus we speak sometimes of correcting A — construed as a mistake — and other times of learning or violating A — construed as a rule or fact about English grammar.

This means that there is another side of the definition of hierarchy. Thinking of the elements in the hierarchy as rules instead of mistakes as above leads us to redefine it thus:

> A is higher in the hierarchy than B is violating A makes sentence comprehension more difficult than violating B.

This leaves open a very important question. Given that A is higher in the comprehensibility hierarchy than B, what is the relationship between learning A and learning B? To answer this question we would seek cases where learning A is easier than learning B, or learning A makes it easier to learn B, or where learning A makes it possible to postpone teaching B because the sentence resulting from correcting A isn't so bad. There are some examples of these cases, but a detailed study of them is beyond the scope of this paper.

To determine what kinds of mistakes make sentence comprehension more difficult, we took a mangled sentence or paragraph and corrected one mistake at a time, holding the rest of the sentence constant. Then we compared sentences where one mistake or combination of mistakes was corrected with the same sentence where another mistake (or combination) was corrected. We then tried to determine which correction made the sentence sound the best, by asking many native speakers with no interest in the outcome. Below, we present examples of mistakes corrected hierarchically.

2.0 *Global and local mistakes*

In studying example after example, we find that mistakes fall into two major classes. Global mistakes are those that violate rules involving the overall structure of a sentence, the relations among constituent clauses, or, in a simple sentence, the relations among major constituents. Local mistakes cause trouble in a particular constituent, or in a clause of a complex sentence. These are relative notions; something that is global in one sentence may become local when that sentence is embedded in a bigger sentence.

We have found that global mistakes are higher on the hierarchy than local ones. Thus, a sentence with both global and local mistakes improves much more when a global mistake is corrected than a local one, or even a group of local ones. Most typical of global mistakes are those which confuse the relationship among clauses, such as:

1. use of connectors, especially meaningful ones,
2. distinctions between co-ordinate and relative clause constructions,
3. parallel structure in reduced co-ordinate clauses,
4. tense continuity across clauses.

These are much more important to general sentence comprehensibility than any corrections within a single clause of the same (complex) sentence such as agreement, articles, noun phrase formation, etc. The hypothesis that follows rather naturally from this observation is this:

HYPOTHESIS: In sentences with more than one clause, the appropriate overall organization is more important to comprehensibility than the correct formation of each clause within the larger sentence.

We will now provide examples illustrating the importance of global mistakes such as 1-4 above, as compared with the lesser importance of local corrections.

Examples of 1: Presence, correctness, and placement of appropriate meaning-bearing connectors outweighs most local corrections.

Let us now consider an example of this:

First example of 1:

#I didn't like took it, but my friend said *that not take this bus, we are late for school.*[2]

Consider only the italicized clauses. We first correct the local mistakes in each clause:

CLAUSE 1: *that not take this bus*

Local Mistakes	Correction	Corrected Result
subject missing	supply *we*	...that we not take...
auxiliary missing	supply *do*	...that we do not take...

CLAUSE 2: *we are late for school*

wrong tense	supply *will*	...we will be late...

This gives us:

...that we do not take this bus we will be late for school.

Adding the missing connector does more for the sentence, though:

...if not take this bus, we are late for school.

As another example, consider this sentence:

Second example of 1:

I should like know, if have taken your course intermediate in May, in September I shall be able get through TOEFEL examination, and I shall be able to enter in the University in September, owing to which I losted two semester and I should like not lost other semester.

Let us first consider the local problems in just the first four clauses, up to *owing to which*:

CLAUSE 1: *I should like know*

Local Mistakes	Correction	Corrected Result
to is missing in infinitive	insert *to*	I should like to know...

CLAUSE 2: *if have taken your course intermediate in May*

Local Mistakes	Correction	Corrected Result
subject is missing	insert *I*	...if I have...
noun-adjective order	invert	...your intermediate course...

CLAUSE 3: *in September I shall be able get through TOEFEL examination*

to missing before infinitive	insert *to*	. . .I shall be able to get through. . .
article missing	insert *the*	. . .get through the TOEFEL. . .

CLAUSE 4: *and I shall be able to enter in the University in September*

extra *in*	delete *in*	. . .enter the University. . .

If we correct every local mistake in each of the first four clauses, we have:

> I should like to know, if I have taken your intermediate course in May in September I shall be able to get through the TOEFEL examination, and I shall be able to enter the University in September. . .

This improves the sentence somewhat, but only insofar as each clause is itself correctly formed. But the sentence still sounds somehow disjointed because the relation between the clauses is obscured. If we now correct for connectors, by inserting *whether* before clauses three and four, and leave all the local mistakes uncorrected, we have:

> I should like know, if have taken your course intermediate in May, whether in September I shall be able get through TOEFEL examination and whether I shall be able to enter in the University in September. . .

The meaning of this sentence is much easier to grasp in one reading than when all the local mistakes were corrected. Again, the importance of having the correct connectors becomes clear. Consider now the last two clauses:

CLAUSE 5: *owing to which I losted two semester*

Local Mistakes	*Correction*	*Corrected Result*
incorrect past tense form	replace by *lost*	. . .owing to which I lost. . .
semester should be plural	replace by *semesters*	. . .owing to which I lost two semesters. . .

CLAUSE 6: *I should like not lost other semester*

lost should be *to lose*	insert correct infinitive	. . .and I should like not to lose. . .
not is in wrong place	put *not* before *like*	. . .and I should not like to lose. . .
article missing	insert *the*	. . .and I should not like to lose the other. . .

If we correct all the local mistakes in these clauses, we are left with:

> . . .(able to enter the University in September) owing to which I lost two semesters and I should not like to lose the other semester.

Again, although the clauses are each well-formed, their relationship, especially to the first part of the sentence, is unclear. But if we take out the wrong subordinate connector *owing to which* and replace it by the correct connector *because,* making no local corrections, the meaning of the clauses and their relation to the rest of the sentence becomes instantly clear:

...(able to enter in the University in September) *because* I losted two semester and I should like not lost other semester.

Examples of 2: Correct distinction between co-ordinate and relative clauses outweighs errors within conjuncts.

As an example of 2, consider this sentence:

#Then at 2:30 Mr. Burthlay being the most kind person and has a fill of humility in nature, in fact I will say he is the most kind staff of humorous in the college and is in charge of the English language, showed his humanitarian to the crowd...

There are quite a number of lexical mistakes in all these clauses.

CLAUSE 2: *and has a fill of humility in nature*

Local Mistakes	Correction	Corrected Result
has a fill of humility in nature	has a humble nature	...and has a humble nature...

CLAUSE 3: *he is the most kind staff of humorous in the college*

staff of humorous	humorous staff member	...he is the most kind, humorous staff member...

CLAUSE 5: *showed his humanitarian to the crowd*

humanitarian	humanitarian-ism	...showed his humanitarianism to the crowd...

These local mistakes all corrected leave us with:

Then at 2:30 Mr. Burthlay being the most kind person and has a humble nature, in fact I will say he is the most kind, humorous staff member in the college and is in charge of the English language, showed his humanitarianism to the crowd...

This is better, but the problem conjunction still leaves the whole last half of the sentence feeling quite strange. If we correct only this and no local mistakes, the sentence sounds more connected than if we correct just the local mistakes:

...in fact I will say he is the most kind staff of humorous in the college who is in charge...

This is already an improvement, but we can go one step further. The preferred constituent order dictates that the relative clause must

immediately follow its antecedent head noun, *Mr. Burthlay.*
This correction gives:

> ...Mr. Burthlay, who is in charge of the English language, being the most kind person...

These two corrections together improve the sentence more than all the local mistakes.

Example of 3: Parallel structure in reduced coordinate clauses is more important than correct formation of each clause.

> #I should like your holding open a place and that you send an application.

The only problem with this sentence is that each clause has the wrong complementizer. *Your holding open* should be *you to hold open*, and *that you send* should be *to send*:

> I should like you to hold open a place and to send an application.

Notice, however, that the global question of conformity between complementizers of conjoined sentences (i.e., parallel structure) is more important than the correct complementizer choice in either of the conjoined clauses. The following sentences still sound better than the original:

> I should like that you hold open a place and that you send an application.

> I should like your holding open a place and your sending an application.

In this particular case of 3, then, parallel structure outweighs correct complementizer choice.

Example of 4: Tense continuity across clauses outweighs local corrections within clauses.

The local mistakes for the following sentence:

> #My friend said that not take this bus, we are late for school.

were cited on page 74. If these corrections are made in either clause, the sentence does improve somewhat. However, the correct sequence of tenses across clauses adds more to the comprehensibility of the sentence than corrections made within either clause:

> ...said that didn't take this bus, would be late for school.

3.0 *In the Skeleton of the Clause*

We can generalize our hypothesis about complex sentences to cover sentences which are "simple" in that they consist of only one clause. It is not simply among clauses that relations must be clear, but more generally among constituents. The major signal English uses to express relations among major constituents is word order. Without an explicit signal to the contrary, we expect to see a subject, then a verb, then an object. After that can come various adverbial phrases. One of the most obvious ways to confuse the intended relations is to confuse the order of subject and object. For example:

English language use much people.

Correcting each constituent, locally, gives

The English language uses many people.

This improvement is negligible compared with the global correction of the word order:

Much people use English language.

Another common way students have of obscuring the meaning of a sentence is to intrude material between the verb and object, making us "hunt" for the object. Example:

Please sending when you shall to get my visa.

From the context of this sentence it was clear that the student was requesting his visa, not the date when someone would get the visa. So the most important correction here is to put the direct object directly after the verb:

Please sending my visa when you shall to get.

There is still a lot wrong with this sentence but this is the most effective single correction, as may be seen by trying the other possibilities.

Our research shows how the overall structure of sentences, whether simple or complex, outweighs the structure of each constituent. The preceding section shows that relations among clauses outweigh formation of each clause; here we see the major constituent relations of simple sentences outweigh formation of each constituent. Since the clauses in a complex sentence are themselves major constituents, a single rule can cover both cases:

Relations among major constituents outweigh formation of each constituent.

This step-by-step correction of badly formed sentences seeks to establish two points: first, that some mistakes are more important to correct than others, and second, that the correction of global mistakes in particular is more important than that of local ones, and gives more satisfaction.

4.0 *The Hierarchy and Teaching*

There is still a fundamental question to be asked. What is the correlation between pointing out global mistakes (or local ones) and students learning to correct them? Is it easier for students to learn to correct global or local mistakes? We claim that it is easier to make a student appreciate and correct a global error. In the following sentence, for example:

Because the harvest be good, there rained enough.

is it easier to get him to say

A. The harvest be good because their rained enough.

where the global mistake has been corrected, or does he more easily say:

B. Because the harvest was good, it rained enough.

where the local mistakes have been corrected? The hierarchy; of course, would dictate that we teach him to say A before B, since the meaning of A is clear, but the meaning of B is not. There is some evidence to suggest that students learn to say A more readily than B. The reason we suggest for this involves a distinction between first and second language learning.

Candidates for global mistakes, such as connectors (*and, but*), subordinating conjunctions (*because, although, after, if-then*) and the position of main and subordinate clauses often have semantic equivalents in other languages. But many times students just don't know enough of the language to know what to do with it. For students with special problems, we have tried this method: for sentences such as the one just cited, where *because* is put before the wrong clause, we found the student's word for *because* and put it before a wrong clause in his language. The strangeness of the result made him see the gravity (for comprehension) of the mistake he made in English and he corrected it.

One cannot predict who is going to make global mistakes, but we can predict that everyone will make local ones. Perhaps the reason this method works with global mistakes is that people are not used to hearing speakers of their own language, not even children, making global mistakes. But local mistakes, i.e., simple kinds of grammar mistakes, do not seem as surprising because children learning the language make them. Even adults make them.

So, it may be possible to extend the distinction between global and local mistakes to a distinction between first and second language learning:

Global mistakes may occur in some instances of second language learning, but they do not occur in first language learning.

This article is published for the first time in this volume.

FOOTNOTES

[1]The symbol # denotes the type of sentence actually spoken by students learning English.

[2]The sentences as we quote them are in many cases taken out of a larger context, which made the intended meaning clearer than they may seem here.

9.
IMITATION AND CORRECTION IN FOREIGN LANGUAGE LEARNING[1]

FREDA M. HOLLEY & JANET K. KING

1.0 *Introduction*

The aim of this article is to explore the degree to which accepted methods of correction may contribute to poor student performance and suggest modifications of current practices. Our suggestions rest on the conviction that student communication in the foreign language may be actively discouraged by the instructor who insists upon grammatical accuracy. Recent linguistic data supports the thesis that overt correction is unnecessary and, indeed, inadvisable. The approach we present is based on recent studies of first language acquisition coupled with conclusions based on evaluation of video tapes. The tapes in question were made in conjunction with a graduate course in applied linguistics and the teaching of German.[2]

Current teaching practices are based largely on the assumption that children learn languages by imitation and that this process can be reproduced in the classroom through memorization of dialogs and pattern drill.[3] Most textbooks give rote drill or imitative learning a significant role. Foreign language teachers have been trained to correct faulty student responses quickly and consistently for grammatical or pronunciation errors assuming that correct learning will result.

The validity of these assumptions seems arguable. Jakobovits has suggested that students' inability to speak the foreign language may be due to their teachers' unreasonably high demands.[4] Cook proposes that the foreign language teacher's classroom expectations do not reflect the ways in which a child apparently acquires language.[5]

Recent work in the field of child language acquisition indicates that a child does not learn to speak purely by imitating adults and subsequently bringing those imitations into closer and closer approximation of the adult utterances. Instead, the child is viewed as forming hypotheses about the language he hears and developing his own grammar in successive stages.[6] Rather than simply repeating parrot-like, the child apparently modifies his operational grammar to approximate the adult speech he hears.

Using Ervin's data on children's past tense formation in English, McNeill points out that children learned correct forms of strong verbs very early only apparently to "unlearn" them after adding weak verb inflection to their grammars.[7] Evidently the repetition practice which these children did with irregular forms was less significant to them than the regular weak verb pattern acquired later. Cook suggests that the view in second language teaching is almost the reverse—practice is considered the most important component in second language learning. She cautions that perceiving patterns may be considerably more important than practice. This definitely seems to be true for a child's language acquisition.[8]

Of course, children are aware of disparities between their own and the adult grammar. A study by Shipley, Smith, and Gleitman indicated that children at one state respond best to commands which exemplify the next level in their language development.[9] A two-year-old capable of one word utterances responded best to "telegraphic" commands such as "Throw ball," characteristic of children at the next stage where sentence length is around two words. The two-and-one-half to three-year-olds, on the other hand, responded best to well-formed commands such as "Throw me the ball" even though they were themselves producing telegraphic utterances of the "Throw ball" type. Yet each group tended to be unresponsive to utterances which were more than one level beyond their production. Logically, correction done at a level beyond the children's comprehension would find them equally unresponsive.

The traditional view that children learn language through correction by their mothers and adults in general is subject to other qualifications as well. Apparently mothers reinforce incorrect statements as frequently as they do correct ones.[10] Significantly, content counts rather than grammar: utterances that are factually correct or appropriate are reinforced whether or not they are grammatically correct. The child's demand of "cuk" may draw an expanded version from the mother ("Do you want a cookie?"), but the child does not have to produce the correct forms to get his cookie.

Unlike the second language learner, the child has a great deal of freedom to make mistakes in his development toward an adult grammar. The only constraint imposed on the child's production is that he must communicate his needs and wishes. Unlike the second language learner, there is no stigma attached to the child's grammatical mistakes. Negative or positive responses from others are almost always based on the content of a child's response rather than the grammatical form.

A child is also allowed much more freedom to play with language than is the second language learner. Not only is he freer in the home, but much of his early practice comes in play situations with other children whose grammars are also incomplete, or by adult standards, inaccurate.

Cazden followed the verbal development of two groups of lower class Negro children, each of which received different verbal support from adult teachers. In one group the teacher consistently expanded (thereby correcting) the children's utterances; in the other the teacher consistently modeled new structures for the children. The second group progressed more rapidly.[11]

Certainly the evidence on child acquisition of language should stimulate the foreign language teacher to rethink current classroom practices, particularly those connected with correction of student utterances. A case can be made for permitting and even encouraging foreign language students to produce sentences that are ungrammatical in terms of full native competence. This would allow the learner to progress, like the child, by forming a series of increasingly complete hypotheses about the language. Cook has suggested that an emphasis on perception of patterns and verbal play with the language may be more useful than repetition drill. In an experimental class employing micro-teaching we attempted to adapt such views to actual classroom practice.

2.0 *Classroom Approach*[12]

The course in question was composed of graduate students in German. Each week three members of the class taught a coordinated lesson to five or six students. These students had been selected at random from the particular learning level desired. Each teacher had a five minute interval and a specific task upon which subsequent presentations were built. If a first semester dialog was to be taught, the initial five minutes would be devoted to warm-up with group and individual modeling. The next sequence would feature questions and answers over the dialog and, in the last session in the series, the given instructor attempted verbal play and appropriate expansions of resultant student sentences. Thus, if the dialog concerned a new car, the last teacher asked individual students about the cars they drove and attempted to engage the group in a free discussion with emphasis on communicating *content* rather than reproducing correct grammar.

Students were chosen from a first through third year so that the range in ability in the various filmings was considerable. Yet regardless of student ability of the particular teaching task assigned, our teachers consistently overcorrected. As a result they tended to monopolize class time with discourse, explanations without follow-up drill, and lapses into English. In attempting to analyze whether there was a general pattern or correction procedure involved, we adduced the following features:

1. Hesitation on the part of the student was met with immediate provision of a correct response by the teacher.

2. Student responses deemed incorrect by the instructor were cut off before completion, frequently in mid-sentence.

Even with the inhibiting influence of the television camera taken into account, the first television series seemed to be unusually lifeless. We decided to focus our teachers' attention on stimulating class response. The student was encouraged to speak German. The teacher was charged to avoid immediate or obvious reproval of grammatically incorrect answers. Procedures were developed to cope with student hesitation, grammatical inaccuracy, and teacher interruption.

When a student hesitated in answering, the teacher was instructed to say and do nothing for five to ten seconds. If an answer was not forthcoming in that interval, he had several options:

1. Rephrasing the question reducing, when possible, the number of words while consciously emphasizing the so-called contentives rather than the functors, such as prepositions and definite articles.[13] An example is the following exchange:

> Teacher: *Warum ist er denn so spät nach Hause gekommen?*
> Why did he come home so late?
> Student: Er... (hesitation)
> He...
> Teacher: *Warum kommt er spät?*
> Why is he late?

Conversely, we urged teachers to be on the alert for ungrammatical but meaningful answers which could be expanded into correct forms by the instructor:

> Student: *Herr Brown schwimmen.*
> Mr. Brown swims.
> Teacher: *Richtig* (referring to content).
> *Herr Brown geht heute schwimmen.*
> Mr. Brown will go swimming today.

Generally the student was not asked to repeat the expanded form on the theory that his competence was several stages below the longer statement. If the expansion did not reflect his interim grammar he, like the child, would only feel frustrated by a repetition far beyond his ability.

2. Cueing. Instead of supplying the correct answer the teacher was instructed to give hints using grammatical variations of a key content word:

> Student: *Sie hat dort. . .* (Pause)
> She has . . . there
> Teacher: *wohnen, wohnte. . .*
> live, lived. . .
> Student: *gewohnt. Sie hat dort gewohnt..*
> lived. She has lived there—She lived there.

We found that this kind of prompting gave excellent results. Students were almost always able to provide the form in question. Cueing has several other advantages as well. Student response informs the teacher whether or not he is operating within the range of a student's grammar. Perhaps most important is the opportunity for achievement. The student's active participation has a psychological advantage over passive repetition.

3. Generating simple sentences. Here the teacher strives to point out to the entire class that they are capable of creating a number of sentences using the incomplete structure provided by student A:

> Student A: *Sie hat da. . .* (Pause)
> She has. . .there.
> Teacher: *Was kann sie alles machen? Sie hat da. . .*
> What kinds of things can she do? She has. . .
> Student: *geschrieben. Sie hat da geschrieben.*
> written. She has written there/She wrote there.
> Student C: *Sie hat da gesessen.* (and so on)
> She has sat there/She sat there.

Four or five such sentences provide adequate variation and "play" with the language. Personal exchanges stressing content reinforcement can be encouraged by altering the pronoun to the second person:

> Teacher: *Was haben* **Sie** *heute morgen gemacht?*
> What did **you** do this morning?

A class will very quickly adjust to the sentence generating idea. Students unable to answer a very specific question are capable of participation when constraints are eased. By allowing a wider range of acceptable answers the teacher has created learning conditions more comparable to those the child experiences. The student has the alternative of many correct possibilities rather than a highly restricted number.

For teacher training purposes we limited our remedial suggestions to rephrasing (reduction or expansion with emphasis on contentives), cueing, and sentence generation. In over fifty percent of the instances filmed, neither corrective measure was needed. The teacher's pause and its concomitant non-verbal expectation of student performance seemed to create a class atmosphere conducive to response. Moreover, the time interval allowed students did not produce as much tension as the practice by which the teacher supplied correct answers. Pauses did not slow the tempo of the lesson noticeably. We concluded that teacher correction, explanation, and the restatements of questions take up as much or more class time than the extra seconds of silence.

3.0 Guidelines

How does the instructor create a situation in which the student can make grammatical mistakes without onus and still be encouraged to evaluate and accept or reject his own linguistic hypotheses? The following guidelines were suggested:

1. The instructor is to allow a student to complete his statement, albeit incorrectly, without interruption.

2. The teacher is asked to model any incorrect student response, substituting grammatically correct forms where necessary. However, he is not to call attention to the correction in any other way. Students are to be commended for expressing ideas in the foreign language. The following exchange illustrates the approach:

> Teacher: *Wem gehört das Auto?*
> To whom does the car belong?
> Student: *Das war ihres Auto.*
> That was her car.
> Teacher: *Ja. Das was ihr Auto.*
> Yes. That was her car.

The instructor praises the statement's *factual* accuracy. He does not call attention to the grammatically incorrect adjective ending *ihres*.

Television replays confirmed the fact that normal corrective procedures confuse the student. He fails to perceive the distinction between the accuracy of communication and the innaccuracy of grammar production. For example, if our teacher in the foregoing situation had responded by saying *"Nein. Das war ihr Auto,"* the student would probably have been as uncertain about his communicative ability as he was about his grammar. The child language learner and his adult counterpart in the foreign country generally share an advantage which the classroom student is denied: the former is corrected almost exclusively with reference to the intelligibility of his utterances whereas the classroom learner generally hears about his grammatical mistakes, not whether anyone can understand what he is saying.

Unavoidably, demands for grammatical accuracy are in direct conflict with unhampered student use of the foreign language. This conflict can be minimized, however, by placing stringent conditions on the form of correction and the circumstances under which correction is advisable. Our graduate students were told that the error had to be common to the group as a whole and/or reflect material being taught in the actual lesson. The instructor was to address corrective procedures to the class rather than to a particular individual. Explanations were to be followed either by drill or, preferably, visual models which serve as the basis for generating sentences.

In a lesson introducing modal auxiliaries, student difficulty with word order was handled in the following manner:

Teacher: Remember with a modal the second verb is at the end of the clause as in these examples: (On the blackboard or an overhead projector)

Er kann heute studieren.
He can study today.

Wir müssen Chemie lernen.
We must learn chemistry.

Du sollst jetzt. . . (to be completed)
You should . . . now.

Er will nicht. . .
He doesn't want to. . .

The teacher in this instance did not provide a complete explanation of German word order with the use of modals. Instead, the class was presented with an interim rule which will have to be modified later when the perfect tenses or transposed word order are introduced. Too often correction involves confronting the student with the complete rules of fully native competence not allowing him to modify his comprehension in a sequence of stages as the child is apparently able to do. By eliciting student responses as the basis of blackboard models the instructor has suggested the boundaries within which the class can play with the language and experiment with the given, admittedly incomplete, hypothesis.

Students were encouraged to develop their ability to discriminate between grammatically correct and incorrect forms by the simple expedient of selecting one of two versions modeled by the instructor. The teacher might ask, for example:

> *"Was sagt man auf deutsch? Wir können singen das Lied?* [*oder*]
> What does one say in German? We can the song sing? [or]
>
> *Wir können das Lied singen? "*
> We can sing the song?

Seven times out of the eleven instances noted students were able to identify correct usage by the teacher although they were unable to actually produce these forms themselves.

Underlying the foregoing procedures is the assumption that stringent demands for grammatical accuracy are not only unrealistic but possibly harmful in learning a second language. Rather than engaging in overt correction of individual students, teacher assistance should be geared toward enabling the class to discover what it can do correctly within specified limits. Student errors should be dealt with as a necessary feature of experimentation in the language. Such experimentation may be as important as repetition practice, if not more so. As is true of the child in his home and the adult language learner in a foreign country, successful exchange of ideas should be valued and rewarded whether these ideas are expressed grammatically or not.

We were satisfied that techniques based on these assumptions produced greater participation and interaction between the classes and the instructors televised. It remains to be studied whether over an extended period of time students actually learn more in a classroom oriented around these practices.

Reprinted from *Modern Language Journal*, Vol. 55, No. 8, by permission of the authors and publishers.

FOOTNOTES

[1]During the preparation of this article Mrs. Holley was supported by a United States Office of Education Fellowship. The authors wish to thank Carlota S. Smith for her suggestions and criticism in regard to the linguistic and psycholinguistic aspects of this article.

[2]Our thanks to the Communication Center at the University of Texas at Austin and in particular Mr. Bill Thompson, Texas Education Microwave Project and Closed Circuit Television Coordinator.

[3]Robert Lado, *Language Teaching* (New York: McGraw-Hill, 1964), pp. 61-62.

[4]Leon A. Jakobovits, "Research Findings and Foreign Language Requirements in College and Universities," *Foreign Language Annals,* II (1969), p. 445.

[5]Vivian Cook, "The Analogy between First and Second Language Learning," *International Review of Applied Linguistics,* VII (1969), pp. 207-216.

[6]Of course it would be misleading to imply that anyone knows how children acquire language. Susan Ervin examines the major theories: (1) imitation of adult sentences with gradual elimination of abbreviations and errors; (2) comprehension of adult rules but random errors in speaking; (3) successive systems with increasing complexity. She concludes that "in their simplest forms all these positions seem wrong. . ." but that the third comes closest to the truth in that "any system of analysis which omits either the idiosyncratically structured and rule-governed features of children's language or the gradual changes within these rules is contradicted by evidence from all levels of linguistic behavior in children." See "Imitation in Children's Language," in *New Directions in the Study of Language,* edited by Eric H. Lenneberg (Cambridge, Massachusetts: M.I.T. Press, 1967), pp. 184-188.

[7]David McNeil, "Developmental Psycholinguistics," in *The Genesis of Language,* edited by George Miller and Frank Smith (Cambridge, Massachusetts: M.I.T. Press, 1966), pp. 70-71.

[8]Cook, p. 216.

[9]E. F. Shipley, Carlota S. Smith, and Lila R. Gleitman, "A Study in the Acquisition of Language: Free Responses to Commands," *Language,* 45 (1969), pp. 322-342.

[10]Roger Brown and Ursula Bellugi, "Three Processes in the Child's Acquisition of Syntax," in *New Directions in the Study of Language,* edited by Eric H. Lenneberg (Cambridge, Massachusetts: M.I.T. Press, 1967), pp. 143-144.

[11]Courtney B. Cazden, "Environmental Assistance to the Child's Acquisition of Syntax," Unpublished dissertation (Harvard, 1965).

[12]Although the experience we cite is based on work with first year college students, the linguistic data suggest our proposals would be equally valid at the high school and elementary school level.

[13]Brown and Bellugi make this distinction in the following terms: "Forms likely to be retained are nouns and verbs and, less often, adjectives, and these are the three large and 'open' parts of speech in English. The number of forms in any one of these parts of speech is extremely large and always growing. Words belonging to these classes are sometimes called 'contentives' because they have semantic content. Forms likely to be omitted are inflections, auxiliary verbs, articles, prepositions, and conjunctions. These forms belong to syntactic classes that are small and closed. Any one class has few members, and new members are not readily added. The omitted forms are the ones that linguists sometimes call 'functors,' their grammatical *functions* being more obvious than their semantic content" (p. 139).

h.
THE SIGNIFICANCE
OF LEARNER'S ERRORS

S. P. CORDER

1.0 *Introduction*

When one studies the standard works on the teaching of modern languages it comes as a surprise to find how cursorily the authors deal with the question of learners' errors and their correction. It almost seems as if they are dismissed as a matter of no particular importance, as possible annoying, distracting, but inevitable by-products of the process of learning a language about which the teacher should make as little fuss as possible. It is of course true that the application of linguistic and psychological theory to the study of language learning added a new dimension to the discussion of errors; people now believed they had a principled means for accounting for these errors, namely that they were the result of interference in the learning of a second language from the habits of the first language. The major contribution of the linguist to language teaching was seen as an intensive contrastive study of the systems of the second language and the mother-tongue of the learner; out of this would come an inventory of the areas of difficulty which the learner would encounter and the value of this inventory would be to direct the teacher's attention to these areas so that he might devote special care and emphasis in his teaching to the overcoming, or even avoiding, of these predicted difficulties. Teachers have not always been very impressed by this contribution from the linguist for the reason that their practical experience has usually already shown them where these difficulties lie and they have not felt that the contribution of the linguist has provided them with any significantly new information. They noted for example that many of the errors with which they were familiar were not predicted by the linguist anyway. The teacher has been on the whole, therefore, more concerned with *how* to deal with these areas of difficulty than with the simple identification of them, and here has reasonably felt that the linguist has had little to say to him.

In the field of methodology there have been two schools of thought in respect of learners' errors. Firstly the school which maintains that if we were to achieve a perfect teaching method the errors would never be committed in the first place, and therefore the occurrence of errors is merely a sign of the present inadequacy of our teaching techniques. The philosophy of the second school is that we live in an imperfect world and consequently errors will always occur in spite of our best efforts. Our ingenuity should be concentrated on techniques for dealing with errors after they have occurred.

Both these points of view are compatible with the same theoretical standpoint about language and language learning, psychologically behaviorist and linguistically taxonomic. Their application to language teaching is known as the audiolingual or fundamental skills. method.

Both linguistics and psychology are in a state at the present time of what Chomsky has called 'flux and agitation' (Chomsky 1966). What seemed to be well established doctrine a few years ago is now the subject of extensive debate. The consequence of this for language teaching is likely to be far reaching and we are perhaps only now beginning to feel its effects. One effect has been perhaps to shift the emphasis away from a preoccupation with *teaching* towards a study of *learning*. In the first instance this has shown itself as a renewed attack upon the problem of acquisition of the mother-tongue. This has inevitably led to a consideration of the question whether there are any parallels between the processes of acquiring the mother-tongue and the learning of a second language. The usefulness of the distinction between acquisition and learning has been emphasized by Lambert (1966) and the possibility that the latter may benefit from a study of the former has been suggested by Carroll (1966).

The differences between the two are obvious but not for that reason easy to explain: that the learning of the mother-tongue is inevitable, whereas, alas, we all know that there is no such inevitability about the learning of a second language; that the learning of the mother-tongue is part of the whole maturational process of the child, while learning a second language normally begins only after the maturational process is largely complete; that the infant starts with no overt language behavior, while in the case of the second language learner such behavior, of course, exists; that the motivation (if we can properly use the term in the context) for learning a first language is quite different from that for learning a second language.

On examination it becomes clear that these obvious differences imply nothing about the *processes* that take place in the learning of first and second language. Indeed the most widespread hypothesis about how languages are learned, which I have called behaviorist, is assumed to apply in both circumstances. These hypotheses are well enough known not to require detailing here, and so are the objections to them. If then these hypotheses about language learning are being questioned and new hypotheses being set up to account for the process of child language acquisition, it would seem reasonable to see how far they might also apply to the learning of a second language.

Within this new context the study of errors takes on a new importance and will I believe contribute to a verification or rejection of the new hypothesis.

This hypothesis states that a human infant is born with an innate predisposition to acquire language; that he must be exposed to language for the acquisition process to start; that he possesses an internal mechanism of unknown nature which enables him from the limited data available to him to construct a grammar of a particular language. How he does this is largely unknown and is the field of intensive study at the present time by linguists and psychologists. Miller (1964) has pointed out that if we wished to create an automaton to replicate a child's performance, the order in which it tested various aspects of the grammar could only be decided after careful analysis of the successive states of language acquisition by human children. The first steps therefore in such a study are seen to be a longitudinal description of a child's language throughout the course of its development. From such a description it is eventually hoped to develop a picture of the procedures adopted by the child to acquire language (McNeill 1966).

The application of this hypothesis to second language learning is not new and is essentially that proposed fifty years ago by H. E. Palmer (1917). Palmer maintained that we were all endowed by nature with the capacity for assimilating language and that this capacity remained available to us in a latent state after the acquisition of a primary language. The adult was seen as capable as the child of acquiring a foreign language. Recent work (Lenneberg 1966) suggests that the child who fails for any reason, i.e. deafness, to acquire a primary language before the age of 12 thereafter rapidly loses the capacity to acquire language behavior at all. This finding does not of course carry with it the implication that the language learning capacity of those who have successfully learned a primary language also atrophies in the same way. It still remains to be shown that the process of learning a second language is of a fundamentally different nature from the process of primary acquisition.

If we postulate the same mechanism, then we may also postulate that the procedures or strategies adopted by the learner of the second language are fundamentally the same. The principal feature that then differentiates the two operations is the presence or absence of motivation. If the acquisition of the first language is a fulfillment of the predisposition to develop language behavior, then the learning of the second language involves the replacement of the predisposition of the infant by some other force. What this consists of is in the context of this chapter irrelevant.

Let us say therefore that, *given motivation*, it is inevitable that a human being will learn a second language if he is exposed to the language data. Study of language aptitude does in some measure support such a view since motivation and intelligence appear to be the two principal factors which correlate significantly with achievement in a second language.

I propose therefore as a working hypothesis that some at least of the *strategies* adopted by the learner of a second language are substantially the same as those by which a first language is acquired. Such a proposal does not imply that the course or *sequence* of learning is the same in both cases.

We can now return to the consideration of errors made by learners. When a two year old child produces an utterance such as "This mummy chair" we do not normally call this deviant, ill-formed, faulty, incorrect or whatever. We do not regard it as an error in any sense at all, but rather as a normal childlike communication which provides evidence of the state of his linguistic development at that moment. Our response to that behavior has certain of the characteristics of what would be called 'correction' in a classroom situation. Adults have a very strong tendency to repeat and expand the child's utterance in an adult version; something like 'Yes, dear, that's Mummy's chair'.

No one expects a child learning his mother-tongue to produce from the earliest stages only forms which in adult terms are correct or non-deviant. We interpret his 'incorrect' utterances as being evidence that he is in the process of acquiring language and indeed, for those who attempt to describe his knowledge of the language at any point in its development, it is the 'errors' which provide the important evidence. As Brown and Frazer (1964) point out the best evidence that a child possesses construction rules is the occurrence of systematic errors, since, when the child speaks correctly, it is quite possible that he is only repeating something that he has heard. Since we do not know what the total input has been we cannot rule out this possibility. It is by reducing the language to a simpler system than it is that the child reveals his tendency to induce rules.

In the case of the second language learner it might be supposed that we *do* have some knowledge of what the input has been, since this is largely within the control of the teacher. Nevertheless it would be wise to introduce a qualification here about the control of input (which is of course what we call the syllabus). The simple fact of presenting a certain linguistic form to a learner in the classroom does not necessarily qualify it for the status of input, for the reason that input is 'what goes in' not what is *available* for going in, and we may reasonably suppose that it is the learner who controls this input, or more properly his intake. This may well be determined by the characteristics of his language acquisition mechanism and not by those of the syllabus. After all, in the mother-tongue learning situation the data available as input is relatively vast, but it is the child who selects what shall be the input.

Ferguson (1966) has recently made the point that our syllabuses have been based at best upon impressionistic judgments and vaguely conceived theoretical principles where they have had any considered foundations at all. The suggestion that we should take more account of the learner's needs in planning our syllabuses is not new, but has not apparently led to any investigations, perhaps because of the methodological difficulties of determining what the learner's needs might actually be. Carroll (1955) made such a proposal when he suggested it might be worth creating a problem-solving situation for the learner in which he must find, by enquiring either of the teacher or a dictionary appropriate verbal responses for solving the problem. He pointed out that such a hypothesis contained certain features of what was believed to occur in the process of language acquisition by the child.

A similar proposal actually leading to an experiment was made Mager but not in connection with language teaching (Mager 1961); it is nevertheless worth quoting his own words:

> 'Whatever sequencing criterion is used it is one which the user calls a 'logical' sequence. But although there are several schemes by which sequencing can be accomplished and, althought it is generally agreed that an effective sequence is one which is meaningful to the learner, the information sequence to be assimilated by the learner is traditionally dictated entirely by the instructor. We generally fail to consult the learner in the matter except to ask him to maximize the effectiveness of whatever sequence we have already decided upon'.

He points out as the conclusions he draws from his small scale experiment that the next step would be to determine whether the learner-generated sequence, or, as we might call it, his *built-in syllabus*, is in some way more efficient than the instructor-generated sequence. It seems entirely plausible that it would be so. The problem is to determine whether there exists such a built-in syllabus and to describe it. It is in such an investigation that the study of learner's errors would assume the role it already plays in the study of child language acquisition, since, as has been pointed out, the key concept in both cases is that the learner is using a definite system of language at every point in his development, although it is not the adult system in the one case, nor that of the second language in the other. The learner's errors are evidence of this system and are themselves systematic.

The use of the term systematic in this context implies, of course, that there may be errors which are random, or, more properly, the systematic nature of which cannot be readily discerned. The opposition between systematic and non-systematic errors is important. We are all aware that in normal adult speech in our native language we are continually committing errors of one sort or another. These, as we have been so often reminded recently, are due to memory lapses, physical states, such as tiredness and psychological conditions such as strong emotion. These are adventitious artifacts of linguistic performance and do not reflect a defect in our knowledge of our own language. We are normally immediately aware of them when they occur and can correct them with more or less complete assurance. It would be quite unreasonable to expect the learner of a second language not to exhibit such slips of the tongue (or pen), since he is subject to similar external and internal conditions when performing in his first or second language. We must therefore make a distinction between those errors which are the product of such chance circumstances and those which reveal his underlying knowledge of the language to date, or, as we may call it his *transitional competence.* The errors of performance will characteristically be unsystematic and the errors of competence, systematic. As Miller (1966) puts it, 'It would be meaningless to state rules for making mistakes'. It will be useful therefore hereafter to refer to errors of performance as *mistakes*, reserving the term *error* to refer to the systematic errors of the learner from which we are able to reconstruct his knowledge of the language to date, i.e. his *transitional competence.*

Mistakes are of no significance to the process of language learning.

However, the problem of determining what is a learner's mistake and what a learner's error is one of some difficulty and involves a much more sophisticated study and analysis of errors than is usually accorded them.

A learner's errors, then, provide evidence of the system of the language that he is using (i.e. has learned) at a particular point in the course (and it must be repeated that he is using some system, although it is not yet the right system). They are significant in three different ways. First to the teacher, in that they tell him, if he undertakes a systematic analysis, how far towards the goal the learner has progressed and, consequently, what remains for him to learn. Second, they provide to the researcher evidence of how language is learned or acquired, what strategies or procedures the learner is employing in his discovery of the language. Thirdly (and in a sense this is their most important aspect) they are indispensible to the learner himself, because we can regard the making of errors as a device the learner uses in order to learn. It is a way the learner has of testing his hypotheses about the nature of the language he is learning. The making of errors then is a strategy employed both by children acquiring their mother-tongue and by those learning a second language.

Although the following dialogue was recorded during the study of child language acquisition (Van Buren 1967) it bears unmistakable similarities to dialogues which are a daily experience in the second language teaching classroom:

> Mother: Did Billy have his egg cut up for him at breakfast?
> Child: Yes, I showeds him.
> Mother: You what?
> Child: I showed him.
> Mother: You showed him?
> Child: I seed him.
> Mother: Ah, you saw him.
> Child: Yes I saw him.

Here the child, within a short exchange appears to have tested three hypotheses: one relating to the concord of subject and verb in a past tense, another about the meaning of *show* and *see* and a third about the form of the irregular past tense of *see*. It only remains to be pointed out that if the child had answered *I saw him* immediately, we would have no means of knowing whether he had merely repeated a model sentence or had already learned the three rules just mentioned. Only a longitudinal study of the child's development could answer such a question. It is also interesting to observe the techniques used by the mother to 'correct' the child. Only in the case of one error did she provide the correct form herself: *You saw him.* In both the other cases, it was sufficient for her to query the child's utterance in such a form as: *you what?* or *You showed him?* Simple provision of the correct form may not always be the only, or indeed the most effective, form of correction since it bars the way to the learner testing alternative hypotheses. Making a learner try to discover the right form could often be more instructive to both learner and teacher. This is the import of Carroll's proposal already referred to.

We may note here that the utterance of a correct form cannot be taken as proof that the learner has learned the systems which would generate that form in a native speaker, since he may be merely repeating a heard utterance, in which case we should class such behavior, not as language, but in Spolsky's term (Spolsky 1966) 'language-like behavior'. Nor must we overlook the fact that an utterance which is superficially non-deviant is not evidence of a mastery of the language systems which would generate it in a native speaker since such an utterance must be semantically related to the situational context. The learner who produced 'I want to know the English' might have been uttering an unexceptionable sentiment, but it is more likely that he was expressing the wish to know the English language. Only the situational context could show whether his utterance was an error or not.

Although it has been suggested that the strategies of learning a first and second language may be the same, it is nevertheless necessary at this point to posit a distinction between the two. While one may suppose that the first language learner has an unlimited number of hypotheses about the nature of the language he is learning which must be tested (although strong reasons have been put forward for doubting this) we may certainly take it that the task of the second language learner is a simpler one: that the only hypotheses he needs to test are: 'Are the systems of the new language the same or different from those of the language I know?' 'And if different, what is their nature?' Evidence for this is that a large number, but by no means all, of his errors, are related to the systems of his mother-tongue. These are ascribed to interference from the habits of the mother-tongue, as it is sometimes expressed. In the light of the new hypotheses they are best not regarded as the persistence of old habits, but rather as signs that the learner is investigating the systems of the new language. Saporta (1966) makes this point clear, 'The internal structure of the (language acquisition) device, i.e., the learner, has gone relatively unexplored except to point out that one of its components is the grammar of the learner's native language. It has generally been assumed that the effect of this component has been inhibitory rather than facilitative'. It will be evident that the position taken here is that the learner's possession of his native language is facilitative and that errors are not to be regarded as signs of inhibition, but simply as evidence of his strategies of learning.

We have been reminded recently of Von Humboldt's statement that we cannot really teach language, we can only create conditions in which it will develop spontaneously in the mind in its own way. We shall never improve our ability to create such favourable conditions until we learn more about the way a learner learns and what his built-in syllabus is. When we do know this (and the learner's errors will, if systematically studied, tell us something about this) we may begin to be more critical of our cherished notions. We may be able to allow the learner's innate strategies to dictate our practice and determine our syllabus; we may learn to adapt ourselves to *his* needs rather than impose upon him *our* preconceptions of *how* he ought to learn, *what* he ought to learn and *when* he ought to learn it.

Reprinted from *IRAL*, Vol. 5, No. 4, by permission of the author and publishers.

REFERENCES

Brown, R. W. and Fraser, C. "The Acquisition of Syntax," in Ursula Bellugi and Roger Brown (eds). *The Acquisition of Language*, Monograph of the Society for Research in Child Development, Vol. 29 No. 1. 1964.

Carroll, J. B. *The Study of Language*. Harvard University Press, Cambridge 1955.

Carroll, J. B. *Research in Foreign Language Teaching: The Last Five Years*, Report of the Northeast Conference 1966.

Chomsky, N. *Research on Language Learning and Linguistics*, Report of the Northeast Conference 1966.

Ferguson, C. A. *Research on Language Learning. Applied Linguistics*, Report of the Northeast Conference 1966.

Lambert, W. A. "Some Observations on First Language Acquisition and Second Language Learning," (Mimeograph) 1966.

McNeill, D. "Developmental Psycholinguistics," in F. Smith and G. A. Miller (eds). *The Genesis of Language*, The M.I.T. Press. 1966.

Miller, G. A. *The Psycholinguists*, Encounter 23.1. 1964.

Miller, G. A. "Language and Psychology," in E. H. Lenneberg (ed). *New Directions in the Study of Language*, M.I.T. Press. 1966.

Lenneberg, E. H. "The Natural History of Language," in Smith and Miller (eds). *The Genesis of Language*, M.I.T. Press. 1966.

Mager, R. F. "On the Sequencing of Instructional Content," Psychological Reports 1961 (405-412).

Palmer, H. E. "The Principles of Language Study." 1917. Reprinted in *Language and Language Learning*, O.U.P. London 1964.

Spolsky, B. "A Psycholinguistic Critique of Programmed Foreign Language Instruction," *IRAL* 4.2 (119-129).

Saporta, S. "Applied Linguistics and Generative Grammar," in Valdman, A. (ed.). *Trends in Modern Language Teaching*. McGraw-Hill, 1966.

Van Buren, P. Personal communication.

i.
IDIOSYNCRATIC DIALECTS
AND ERROR ANALYSIS

S. P. CORDER

1.0 *Introduction*

What has come to be known as 'Error Analysis' has to do with the investigation of the language of Second-Language learners. I shall be taking the point of view in this chapter that the language of such a learner, or perhaps certain groupings of learners, is a special sort of dialect. This is based on two considerations: firstly, any spontaneous speech intended by the speaker to communicate is meaningful, in the sense that it is systematic, regular and, consequently is, in principle, describable in terms of a set of rules, i.e., it has a grammar. The spontaneous speech of the second-language learner is language and has a grammar. Secondly, since a number of sentences of that language are isomorphic with some of the sentences of his target language and have the same interpretation, then some, at least, of the rules needed to account for the learner's language will be the same as those required to account for the target language. Therefore the learner's language is a dialect in the linguistic sense: two languages which share some rules of grammar are dialects.

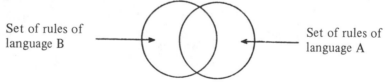

Set of rules of language B → ← Set of rules of language A

Language A and B are in a dialect relation. (I am not here concerned whether or not all languages can be regarded as being in this relation.)

It is, of course, usual to apply a further non-linguistic criterion to a language in order to establish its dialect status, namely that it should be the shared behavior of a social group, i.e., that it should constitute a 'langue' in the Saussurean sense. In this sense the language of a learner may or may not be a dialect. I shall return to this point later. For the time being, however, I shall make a distinction between the dialects which are the languages of a social group (I shall call these social dialects) and the dialects which are not the languages of social groups (I shall call these idiosyncratic dialects). The justification for calling the latter dialects is therefore a linguistic one and not a social one. You may say that the dialects I am talking about are already adequately identified under the name *idiolects*. I would maintain that this is not the case. An idiolect is a personal dialect but which linguistically has the characteristic that all the rules required to account for it are found somewhere in the set of rules of one or another *social* dialect. An *idiolect* can be said to be some sort of a mixture of dialects.

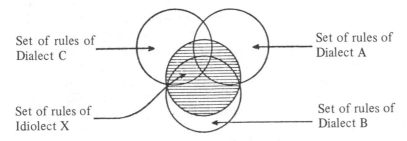

From the diagram we can see that Idiolect X possesses rules drawn from three overlapping social dialects but does not possess any rules which are not rules of any one of these dialects. If all these social dialects are 'included' in a language D then Idiolect X is a dialect of language D in the conventional sense.

This state of affairs is different in the case of what I am calling idiosyncratic dialects. In these, some of the rules required to account for the dialect are not members of the set of rules of any social dialect; they are peculiar to the language of that speaker.

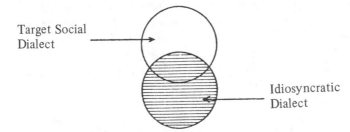

All *idiosyncratic dialects* have this characteristic in common that some of the rules required to account for them are particular to an individual. This has, of course, the result that some of their sentences are not readily interpretable, since the ability to interpret a sentence depends in part upon the knowledge of the conventions underlying that sentence. The sentences of an *idiolect* do not therefore present the same problems of interpretation since somewhere there is a member of that social group who shares the conventions with the speaker.

It is in the nature of *idiosyncratic dialects* that they are normally unstable. The reason for this is obvious. The object of speech is normally to communicate, i.e., to be understood. If understanding is only partial, then a speaker has a motive to bring his behavior into line with conventions of some social group, if he is able. This instability accounts for part of the difficulty experienced by the linguist in describing *idiosyncratic dialects*. The data on which a description is made is fragmentary. This means that the usual verification procedures required in the construction of a projective grammar are not readily available.

The other difficulty the linguist experiences is that of placing an interpretation on some of the sentences of the dialect. Without interpretation, of course, analysis cannot begin.

The language of a second language learner is not the only type of *idiosyncratic dialect*. 'Error Analysis' is not applicable only to the language of second language learners. One class of *idiosyncratic dialects* is the language of poems, where this cannot be accounted for wholly in the terms of the rules of some social dialect. As Thorne (1965) says: "given a text like Cummings' poem 'Anyone lived in a pretty how town' containing sequences which resist inclusion in the grammar of English, it might prove more illuminating to regard it as a sample of a different language, *or a different dialect*, from Standard English" (My italics).

That the language of this poem is idiosyncratic is evident, if only because of the difficulty of interpretation. It is significant that Thorne's approach to the analysis of the language of the poem is essentially that of 'error analysis', a type of bilingual comparison. That is, he attempts to discover the rules which would account for the idiosyncratic sentences[1] in terms of the same syntactic model he uses to account for the social dialect to which it most closely relates: in this case, Standard English.

The idiosyncratic sentences of a poetic text can perhaps with justice be called *deliberately deviant*, since the author presumably knows the conventions of the standard dialect but chooses not to obey them (c.f. Katz 1964). His deviances are motivated. This means that the ability to interpret the text is dependent upon the knowledge of the semantic structure of the related standard dialect. In this sense poetic dialects are 'parasitic' upon standard dialects.

Another idiosyncratic dialect one might consider is the speech of an aphasic. This, too, in the happiest circumstances, is an unstable dialect, but presents the same problem of interpretation to the linguist. Whether it would be just to call the idiosyncratic sentences of an aphasic deviant is, however, less certain. We must assume that he was, before his disease, a native speaker of some social dialect, but he cannot be said to be deviating deliberately, and it is difficult to know in what sense he can be said still to 'know the rules' of the dialect.[2]

Perhaps we may provisionally characterize the idiosyncratic sentences of the aphasic as *pathologically deviant*.

The third class of *idiosyncratic dialects* is that of the infant learning his mother tongue. It too presents typical problems of interpretation, in an even more acute form perhaps, than either of the other two classes. I am open to correction here, but I would guess that the single factor which makes the problem of describing child language so intractable is that of placing a plausible interpretation (let alone a correct interpretation) upon a child's utterances. This idiosyncratic dialect is also obviously unstable.

The fourth class of *idiosyncratic dialects* is that of the learners of a second language. Everything I have said about idiosyncratic dialects in general applies to his language. It is regular, systematic, meaningful, i.e., it has a grammar, and is, in principle, describable in terms of a set of rules, some sub-set of which is a sub-set of the rules of the target social dialect. His dialect is unstable (we hope) and is not, so far as we know, a 'langue' in that its conventions are not shared by a social group, (I shall return to this point later) and lastly, many of its sentences present problems of interpretation to any native speaker of the target dialect. Selinker (1969) has proposed the name *interlanguage* for this class of idiosyncratic dialects, implying thereby that it is a dialect whose rules share characteristics of two social dialects or languages, whether these languages themselves share rules or not. This is an open question and has to do with the problem of language universals.

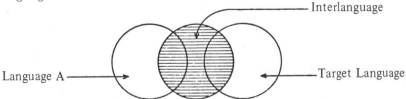

An alternative name might be *transitional dialect*, emphasizing the unstable nature[3] of such dialects.

I have suggested that it would be reasonable to call the idiosyncratic sentences of a poet's dialect *deliberately deviant*, since the writer is assumed to know the conventions of a social dialect and that he deliberately chooses not to follow them. Similarly I have suggested that the aphasic's idiosyncratic sentences might be called *pathologically deviant* since he too was presumably a speaker of some social dialect before his disease. We cannot, however, refer to the idiosyncratic sentences of a child as deviant, since he, of course, is not yet a speaker of a social dialect; and indeed it is not usual (until he goes to school) to call a child's sentences deviant, incorrect or ungrammatical. For precisely the same reason I suggest it is misleading to refer to the idiosyncratic sentences of the second language learner as *deviant*. I also suggest that it is as undesirable to call them *erroneous* as it is to call the sentences of a child erroneous, because it implies willful, or inadvertent breach of rules which, in some sense, ought to be known. Whereas, of course, sentences are idiosyncratic precisely because the rules of the target dialect are not yet known.

The only sentences in anyone's speech which could, I suggest, with justice be called *erroneous* are those which are the result of some failure of performance. These may contain what are often called slips of the tongue, false starts, changes of mind, and so on. Hockett (1948) refers to these as lapses. They may be the result of failures in memory. A typical example in English would be: "That is the problem which I don't know how to solve it" (Reibel 1969). Interestingly such erroneous sentences do not normally present problems of interpretation. The reason that suggests itself for this is that there may be, in any social dialect, 'rules for making mistakes'. Here, clearly, is a field for investigation (Boomer and Laver, 1968). But we are not yet in a position, I think, to set up a fifth class of idiosyncratic dialects to account for the regularities of erroneous sentences. The noticeable thing about *erroneous* sentences is that they are normally readily corrected or correctable by the speaker himself. This could be a defining criterion for erroneous sentences. It would, of course, be applicable to some sentences of the second language learner. Such sentences could be accounted for as being cases of *failure* (for whatever reason) to follow a *known* rule, in contradistinction to what I am calling idiosyncratic sentences, which involve no failure in performance and which cannot be corrected by the learner precisely because they follow the only rules known to him, those of his transitional dialect.

But so long as we do not make the mistake of assuming that the idiosyncratic sentences of a learner of a second-language are simply the result of performance failure, that is, that he knows the rules of the target language but has, for some reason or other failed to, or chosen not to, apply them, then there is no harm in talking about *error* or *correction.*

My principal reason for objecting to the terms *error, deviant* or *ill-formed* is that they all, to a greater or lesser degree, prejudge the explanation of the idiosyncrasy. Now, one of the principal reasons for studying the learner's language is precisely to discover why it is as it is, that is, to explain it and ultimately say something about the learning process. If, then, we call his sentences deviant or erroneous, we have implied an explanation before we have ever made a description.

There is an even more compelling reason for not calling the idiosyncratic sentences of a learner *ungrammatical.* While it is true that they cannot be accounted for by the rules of the target dialect, they are in fact *grammatical* in terms of the learner's language.

I have suggested that the idiosyncratic dialects I have identified differ from social dialects in that some of the rules needed to account for them are not members of the set of rules of any social dialect, that they are in fact idiosyncratic rules, not shared rules. It is, however, possible that while these dialects are not 'langues', in the sense that their conventions are not shared by any social group identifiable according to the criteria of the sociologist, nevertheless the idiosyncratic rules are not unique to an individual but shared by others having similar cultural background, aims or linguistic history. Thers is such a term as 'poetic language' or 'poetic dialect' to designate that dialect which possesses certain features found only in poetry. However, such a dialect is part of the 'langue' of the community whose poetry it is and presents no difficulties of interpretation. Such a sentence as: 'And hearkened as I whistled the trampling team beside' is perhaps unique to verse in modern English but can be accounted for by a convention accepted by all English speakers. This is not true, however, of 'Up so many bells. . .' of Cummings' poem. This is not part of the poetic dialect of English, is difficult of interpretation and I doubt whether the rules which accounted for it would account for any other poetic utterances by any other poet. It is fully idiosyncratic.

The situation is, I think, different in the case of the other three classes of idiosyncratic dialects. Aphasics do not form a social group in any sociological sense, and yet there is strong evidence to suggest that the idiosyncracies of their speech may be classified along a number of dimensions (Jakobson, 1956). No one would, of course, attempt to describe the speech of aphasics unless he believed that some general statements of classification were possible. The object of such investigations is to find what relations there are between the medical signs, symptoms, history and the set of rules needed to account for the idiosyncratic aspects of the aphasic's speech.

Similarly, no one would undertake the study of child language acquisition unless he had reason to believe that all children in a certain dialect environment followed a course of development which was more or less similar (Smith and Miller, 1968). There would be little point in describing the speech of *a* three-year-old unless it was expected ultimately to throw light on the speech of *the* three-year-old. Therefore, there is an underlying assumption that the language of all three-year-olds in a certain language environment will have certain features in common.[4]

May it be that the situation is similar in the case of the learner of a second language? It is certainly the case that teachers work on the assumption that a group of learners having the same mother tongue and having had the same experience of learning the second language speak more or less the same interlanguage at any point in their learning career, and that what differences there are can be ascribed to individual variation in intelligence, motivation and perhaps attitude. This belief is inherent in the notion of 'teaching a class' as opposed to an 'individual', and indeed, it is difficult to see how one could proceed otherwise.

Can we assume that such learners all follow a similar course of development in acquiring a second language? We certainly do all we can to see that they do. That is what a syllabus is for. It is a map of the route the learners are to follow. But supposing it were possible for the learner to select his own route, can we assume that he would follow the route we have mapped out for him? We simply do not know, since no one has ever tried to find out. We lack totally any information about the development of individual learners of a second language outside the classroom situation, and indeed it is difficult to imagine how such a study could be made. But one thing is clear: the longitudinal study of the language development of a second language learner would rely heavily upon the techniques of what we are calling 'error analysis' just as the longitudinal study of the infant learning his mother tongue depends on the analysis of his idiosyncratic sentences (Brown and Frazer, 1964). Furthermore, I believe that until we do attempt to undertake the longitudinal study of the free-learning second language learners, we shall not make much headway with finding out how people learn second languages.

I shall now turn to a general consideration of the methodology of describing what I have called an idiosyncratic dialect, and which, in part, is 'error analysis' as we are calling it. I have already suggested that this methodology is not uniquely applicable to the dialects of second-language learners but is valid for all idiosyncratic dialects.

The dialect is *une langue* in the Saussurean sense. It is therefore a methodological mistake to concentrate only on those sentences which are overtly idiosyncratic. The superfically well-formed sentences in terms of one social dialect (the target dialect in the case of the learner) are just as important as those which are overtly idiosyncratic. They too tell us what he knows. Furthermore, as I have suggested above, the 'value' to be assigned to 'well-formed' forms is only discoverable in terms of the whole system of his dialect. Thus, for example, a well-formed 'plural' or an apparently 'proper' use of the definite article can only be understood in relation to his 'ill-formed' plurals or his use of other determiners.

This means that all the learner's sentences should in principle be analyzed. This is all the more necessary since many of his apparently 'well-formed' sentences may have a derivation different from that assigned by the rules of the target dialect. Thus the sentence: 'After an hour it was stopped' was only recognized as idiosyncratic when the context showed that *it* referred to the *wind* and that therefore the target dialect interpretation was unlikely and in fact the translation into the target language was: 'After an hour it stopped'. A similar case in poetic dialect is: 'Anyone lived in a pretty how town' where the syntactic parallel is not with 'Someone lived in a pretty old town' but 'John lived in a pretty old town', i.e., *Anyone* is a proper name in that poetic dialect, and not an indefinite pronoun, and *how* is an adjective and not an interrogative adverb.

The first stage in 'error analysis' then is *recognition of idiosyncracy*. We can enunciate a general law. *Every sentence is to be regarded as idiosyncratic until shown to be otherwise*. As I have suggested, a learner's sentence may be superficially 'well-formed' and yet be idiosyncratic; these sentences I shall call *covertly idiosyncratic*. They may also, of course, be *overtly idiosyncratic*, in that they are superficially 'ill-formed' in terms of the rules of the target language, or they may, of course, be neither. If the 'normal' interpretation is acceptable in context, then that sentence is not for immediate purposes idiosyncratic. If, however, the sentence appears superficially well-formed in terms of the rules of the target language but nevertheless cannot be interpreted 'normally' in context, then that sentence is *covertly idiosyncratic* and a plausible interpretation must be placed upon it in the light of the context. We then have what I call a *reconstructed sentence* to compare with the original. A reconstructed sentence is, roughly speaking, what a native-speaker of the target language would have said to express that meaning in *that* context, i.e., it is a translation equivalent.

Let us take another possibility: that the sentence is *overtly idiosyncratic,* that is, it is superficially 'ill-formed' according to the rules of the target language. We must then ask whether a plausible interpretation can be placed upon it in the context. If it can, well and good, and we can proceed to make a 'well-formed' reconstructed sentence to compare with the original. If we cannot readily make a plausible interpretation of the overtly idiosyncratic sentence then our problem is much greater. Somehow or other we must attempt to make a plausible interpretation. We can first see whether, by reference to the mother-tongue of the learner, we can arrive at such an interpretation. If the mother-tongue is not known then the analysis of that sentence may have to remain in abeyance until we have learned more of the idiosyncratic dialect of the learner. If, however, the mother-tongue is known, we may be able, by a process of literal translation, to arrive at a means of interpreting the sentence plausibly. If we can do that, then, by translating the mother-tongue sentence back into a well-formed sentence of the target language, we have available a reconstructed sentence which once again we can compare with the original overtly idiosyncratic sentence of the learner.

The end point of the process of identifying idiosyncracy and the production of a reconstructed sentence is two sentences: the idiosyncratic sentence and a well-formed sentence, which *by definition* have the same meaning.

I need hardly say that the picture I have given is idealized. At every decision point in the algorithm it is unlikely that a categorical yes/no answer can readily be made. The first decision as to the 'well-formedness' is in itself a problem in view of the intederminacy of grammar (Lyons 1968). But more acute is the problem of interpretation. How can we be sure when interpretation is plausible? Frequently there may be two equally plausible interpretations. Take for example such an overtly idiosyncratic sentence as: *'He didn't know the word so he asked a dictionary.* In the context the interpretation *He asked for a dictionary'* is perhaps as likely as *'He consulted a dictionary'.* There is not always in the context any factor

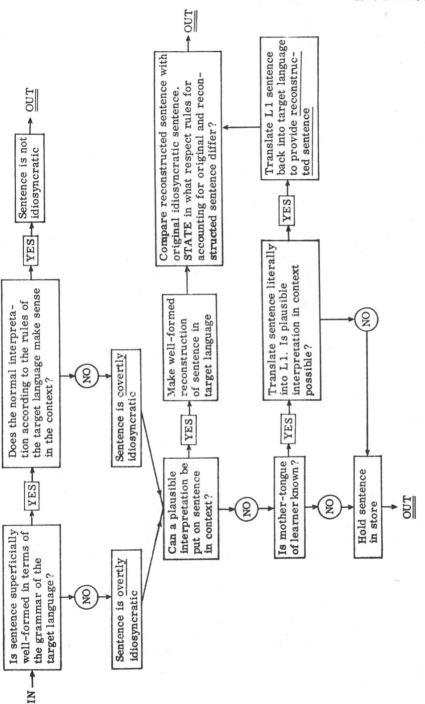

ALGORITHM FOR PROVIDING DATA FOR DESCRIPTION OF IDIOSYNCRATIC DIALECTS

which will make one interpretation more plausible than another. Recourse can often be had to the mother-tongue, if known. But I think it worth pointing out that the problem of interpretation looms larger outside the classroom than in. The teacher has almost certainly learned the idiosyncratic dialect of his class and, of course, there is always the possibility of asking the learner in his mother-tongue to provide an authoritative interpretation.

The recourse to the mother-tongue of the learner (in his absence, that is) is in fact also a highly intuitive process and, of course, depends on the degree of knowledge of that dialect possessed by the investigator. Furthermore, we cannot assume that the idiosyncratic nature of the learner's dialect is solely explicable in terms of his mother-tongue; it may be related to how and what he has been taught. Here again the teacher is in a privileged position to interpret the idiosyncratic sentence, though teachers may be unwilling to admit that idiosyncracy can be accounted for by reference to what they have done or not done!

We have now arrived at the *second state:* accounting for a learner's idiosyncratic dialect. The first stage, if successfully completed, provides us with the data of a set of pairs of sentences which by definition have the same meaning, or put another way, are translation equivalents of each other: one in the learner's dialect, the other in the target dialect. This is the data on which the *description* is based. The methodology of description is, needless to say, fundamentally that of a *bilingual comparison*. In this, two languages are described in terms of a common set of categories and relations, that is, in terms of the same formal model. The technical problems of this are well known and I do not wish, or need, to go into them here.

The *third stage* and ultimate object of error-analysis is *explanation*. Whereas the two previous stages have been linguistic, the third state is psycholinguistic, inasmuch as it attempts to account for how and why the learner's idiosyncratic dialect is of the nature it is. We must, I think, all agree that there could be no reason to engage in error-analysis unless it served one or both of two objects. *Firstly*, to elucidate what and how a learner learns when he studies a second language. This is a theoretical object (Corder 1967); *secondly*, the applied object of enabling the learner to learn more efficiently by exploiting our knowledge of his dialect for pedagogical purposes. The second objective is clearly dependent on the first. We cannot make any *principled* use of his idiosyncratic sentences to improve teaching unless we understand how and why they occur.

It is a generally agreed observation that many — but not necessarily all — the idiosyncratic sentences of a second language learner bear some sort of regular relation to the sentences of his mother tongue.[5]

This is a phenomenon which no one would dispute. It is the explanation of this phenomenon which is open to discussion. One explanation is that the learner is carrying over the habits of the mother tongue into the second language. This is called *interference* and the implication of this term can only be that his mother tongue habits prevent him in some way from acquiring the habits of the second language. Clearly this explanation is related to a view of language as some sort of habit structure.

The other explanation is that language learning is some sort of data-processing and hypothesis-forming activity of a cognitive sort. According to this view his idiosyncratic sentences are signs of false hypotheses, which, when more data is available and processed, either by direct observation or by statements by the teacher, i.e., corrections and examples, enable the learner to reformulate a hypothesis more in accordance with the facts of the target language (c.f. Hockett 1948).

It is not surprising that people holding the habit formation theory of learning, which has been the most prevalent theory over some decades now, showed no particular interest in the study of the learner's idiosyncratic sentences. They were evidence that the correct automatic habits of the target language had not yet been acquired. Their eradication was a matter of more intensive drilling in correct forms. What the nature of the error might be was a matter of secondary importance since it would throw no interesting light on the process of learning. Sufficient that they were there, indicating that the learning task was not yet complete. Theoretically, if the teaching process had been perfect, no errors would have occurred.

The alternative view would suggest that the making of errors is an inevitable and indeed necessary part of the learning process. The 'correction' of error provides precisely the sort of negative evidence which is necessary to discovery of the correct concept or rule. Consequently, a better description of idiosyncratic sentences contributes directly to an account of what the learner knows and does not know at that moment in his career, and should ultimately enable the teacher to supply him, not just with the information *that* his hypothesis is wrong, but also, importantly, with the right sort of information or data for him to form a more adequate concept of a rule in the target language.

It is not, I think, therefore, a pure coincidence that an increased interest in error-analysis at the present time coincides with an increased interest in formulating some alternative hypothesis to the habit-formation theory of language learning.

Reprinted from *IRAL* Vol. 9, No. 2, by permission of the author and publishers.

FOOTNOTES

[1]Strictly speaking, of course, all the sentences of the poem are idiosyncratic, since the dialect is idiosyncratic and as de Saussure says: "la langue est un système dont tous les termes sont solidaires et où la valeur de l'un ne résulte que de la présence simultané des autres". This means that apparently 'non-idiosyncratic' sentences should not receive the same interpretation as they would if they were sentences of Standard English. This is so because the value of any term in a system if a function of all the terms in the system and since by definition his system is different, then the value of all the terms is idiosyncratic, even when surface realization appears the same. I shall, however, hereafter use the term 'idiosyncratic sentence' to refer to any sentence which superficially is not a sentence of any social dialect and also any sentence which, while it superficially resembles a sentence of a social dialect, cannot receive the interpretation that such a sentence would receive in that dialect.

[2]We may note in passing that one of the problems of describing an aphasic's speech is an absence of information about the precise nature of his dialect before illness.

[3]Theoretical objections to the concept of Interlanguage (or Transitional Dialect) apply with equal force to the concept of 'a language'. Both are, of course, unstable. The concept of 'état de langue' underlies all descriptions of languages. The objections to the concept of interlanguage have weight only inasmuch as they are regarded as practical objections to the feasibility of making comprehensive descriptions of an 'état de dialecte', because of the paucity of data available in most cases. The same practical problems beset workers in the field of child language acquisition, of course.

[4]An interesting speculation is whether three-year-olds can understand each other better than adults understand them or than they can understand adult speech.

[5]For an interesting discussion of idiosyncracies which may derive from the methods or materials of teaching or arise in the process of learning from the nature of the target language itself see Richards, (1970).

BIBLIOGRAPHY

Boomer, D.S. and Laver, J.M. *Slips of the Tongue*. B. J. Disorders of Communication III. 1, 1968.

Brown, R. and Frazer "The Acquisition of Syntax" in Bellugi, U. and Brown, R. (eds.): *The Acquisition of Language*, Monograph of the Society for Research in Child Development, Vol. 29, No. 1, 1964.

Corder, S.P. "The Significance of Learners' Errors", *IRAL*, 5, 1967.

Hockett, C.F. "A Note on Structure", *Linguistics* 14, 1948.

Jakobson, R. "Two Aspects of Language and Two Types of Aphasic Disturbance" in *Fundamentals in Language*, 1956.

Katz, J.J. "Semi Sentences" in Fodor, J. A. and Katz J. J., *The Structure of Language*, 1964.

Lyons, J. *Introduction to Theoretical Linguistics*. OUP, 1968.

Reibel, D. A. "What to do with Recalcitrant Relatives", Paper given at the meeting of the Linguistics Association, York, Spring, 1969.

Selinker, L. "Language Transfer" *General Linguistics*, 9, 1969.

Smith and Miller, G.A. *The Genesis of Language*, 1966.

Richards, J. C. *A Non-Contrastive Approach to Error Analysis*. Centre International de Recherches sur le Bilingualisme, 1970.

Thorne, J.P. "Stylistics and Generative Grammars", *Journal of Linguistics*, 1, 1965.

J.
INTERLANGUAGE

LARRY SELINKER

1.0 *Introduction*

This chapter[1] discusses some theoretical preliminaries for researchers concerned with the linguistic aspects of the psychology of second-language learning. These theoretical preliminaries are important because without them it is virtually impossible to decide what data are relevant to a psycholinguistic theory of second-language learning.

It is also important to distinguish between a teaching perspective and a learning one. As regards the 'teaching' perspective, one might very well write a methodology paper which would relate desired output to known inputs in a principled way, prescribing what has to be done by the teacher in order to help the learner achieve learning. As regards the 'learning' perspective, one might very well write a paper describing the process of attempted learning of a second language, successful or not: teaching, textbooks, and other 'external aids' would constitute one, but only one, important set of relevant variables. In distinguishing between the two perspectives,[2] claims about the internal structures and processes of the learning organism take on a very secondary character in the teaching perspective; such claims may not even be desirable here. But such claims do provide the *raison d'être* for viewing the second-language learning from the learning perspective. This chapter is written from the learning perspective, regardless of one's failure or success in the attempted learning of a second language.

In the learning perspective, what would constitute the psychologically-relevant data of second-language learning?[3] My own position is that such data would be those behavioral events which would lead to an understanding of the psycholinguistic structures and processes underlying 'attempted meaningful performance' in a second language. The term 'meaningful performance situation' will be used here to refer to the situation where an 'adult'[4] attempts to express meanings, which he may already have, in a language which he is in the process of learning. Since performance of drills in a second-language classroom is, by definition, not meaningful performance, it follows that from a learning perspective, such performance is, in the long run, of minor interest. Also, behavior which occurs in experiments using nonsense syllables fits into the same category and for the same reason. Thus, data resulting from these latter behavioral situations are of doubtful relevancy to meaningful performance situations, and thus to a theory of second-language learning.

It has long seemed to me that one of our greatest difficulties in establishing a psychology of second-language learning which is relevant to the way people actually learn second languages, has been our inability to identify unambiguously the phenomena we wish to study. Out of the great conglomeration of second-language behavioral events, what criteria and constructs should be used to establish the class of those events which are to count as relevant in theory construction? One set of these behavioral events which has elicited considerable interest is the regular reappearance in second-language performance of linguistic phenomena which were thought to be eradicated in the performance of the learner. A correct understanding of this phenomenon leads to the postulation of certain theoretical constructs, many of which have been set up to deal with other problems in the field. But they also help clarify the phenomenon under discussion. These constructs, in turn, give us a framework within which we can begin to isolate the psychologically-relevant data of second-language learning. The new perspective which an examination of this phenomena gives us is thus very helpful both in an identification of relevant data and in the formulation of a psycholinguistic theory of second-language learning. The main motivation for this chapter is the belief that it is particularly in this area that progress can be made at this time.

2.0 'Interlanguage' and latent structures

Relevant behavioral events in a psychology of second-language learning should be made identifiable with the aid of theoretical constructs which assume the major features of the psychological structure of an adult whenever he attempts to understand second-language sentences or to produce them. If, in a psychology of second-language learning, our goal is explanation of some important aspects of this psychological structure, then it seems to me that we are concerned in large part with how bilinguals make what Weinreich (1953, p. 7) has called 'interlingual identifications'. In his book *Languages in Contact*, Weinreich discusses—though briefly—the practical need for assuming in studies of bilingualism that such identifications as that of a phoneme in two languages, or that of a grammatical relationship in two languages, or that of a semantic feature in two languages, have been made by the individual in question in a language contact situation. Although Weinreich takes up many linguistic and some psychological questions, he leaves completely open questions regarding the *psychological structure* within which we assume 'interlingual identifications' exist; we assume that there is such a *psychological structure* and that it is *latent* in the brain, activated when one attempts to learn a second language.

The closest thing in the literature to the concept *latent psychological structure* is the concept of *latent language structure* (Lenneberg, 1967, especially pp. 374-379) which, according to Lenneberg, (a) is an already formulated arrangement in the brain, (b) is the biological counterpart to universal grammar, and (c) is transformed by the infant into the *realized structure* of a particular grammar in accordance with certain maturational stages. For the purposes of this chapter, I will assume the existence of the latent language structure described by Lenneberg; I shall further assume that there exists in the brain an already formulated arrangement which for most people is different from and exists in addition to Lenneberg's latent language structure. It is important to state that with the latent structure described in this chapter as compared to Lenneberg's, there is no genetic time table;[5] there is no direct counterpart to any grammatical concept such as 'universal grammar'; there is no guarantee that this latent structure will be activated at all; there is no guarantee that the latent structure will be 'realized' into the actual structure of any natural language (i.e., there is no guarantee that attempted learning will prove successful), and there is every possibility that an overlapping exists between this latent language acquisition structure and other intellectual structures.

The crucial assumption we are making here is that those adults who 'succeed' in learning a second language so that they achieve native-speaker 'competence' have somehow reactivated the *latent language structure* which Lenneberg describes. This absolute success in a second language affects, as we know from observation, a small percentage of learners—perhaps a mere 5%. It follows from this assumption that this 5% go through very different psycholinguistic processes than do most second-language learners and that these successful learners may be safely ignored—in a counterfactual sense[6]—for the purposes of establishing the constructs which point to the psychologically-relevant data pertinent to most second-language learners. Regarding the study of the latter group of learners (i.e., the vast majority of second-language learners who fail to achieve native-speaker competence), the notion of 'attempted learning' is independent of and logically prior to the notion of 'successful learning'. In this chapter, we will focus on attempted learning by this group of learners, successful or not, and will assume that they activate a different, though still genetically determined structure (referred to here as the *latent psychological structure*) whenever they attempt to produce a sentence in the second-language, that is whenever they attempt to express meanings, which they may already have, in a language which they are in the process of learning.

This series of assumptions must be made, I think, because the second-language learner who actually achieves native-speaker competence cannot possibly have been taught this competence, since linguists are daily—in almost every generative study—discovering new and fundamental facts about particular languages. Successful learners, in order to achieve this native-speaker competence, must have acquired these facts (and most probably important principles of language organization) *without* having explicitly been taught them.[7]

Regarding the ideal second-language learner who will *not* 'succeed' (in the absolute sense described above) and who is thus representative of the vast majority of second-language learners, we can idealize that from the beginning of his study of a second language, he has his attention focused upon one norm of the language whose sentences he is attempting to produce. With this statement, we have idealized the picture we wish to sketch in the following ways:[8] the generally accepted notion 'target language' (TL), i.e., the second-language the learner is attempting to learn, is here restricted to mean that there is only one norm of one dialect within the interlingual focus of attention of the learner. Furthermore, we focus our analytical attention upon *the only observable data to which we can relate theoretical predictions:*[9] the utterances which are produced when the learner attempts to say sentences of a TL. This set of utterances for *most* learners of a second language is not identical to the hypothesized corresponding set of utterances which would have been produced by a native speaker of the TL had he attempted to express the same meaning as the learner. Since we can observe that these two sets of utterances are not identical, then in the making of constructs relevant to a theory of second-language learning, one would be completely justified in hypothesizing, perhaps even *compelled* to hypothesize, the existence of a separate linguistic system[10] based on the observable output which results from a learner's attempted production of a TL norm. This linguistic system we will call 'interlanguage' (IL).[11] One of the main points of this paper is the assumption that predictions of behavioral events in a theory of second-language learning should be primarily concerned with the linguistic shapes of the utterances produced in ILs. Successful predictions of such behavioral events in meaningful performance situations will add credence to the theoretical constructs related to the latent psychological structure discussed in this chapter.

It follows from the above that the only observable data from meaningful performance situations we can establish as relevant to interlingual identifications are: (1) utterances in the learner's native language (NL) produced by the learner; (2) IL utterances produced by the learner; and (3) TL utterances produced by native speakers of that TL. These three sets of utterances or behavioral events are, then, in this framework, the psychologically-relevant data of second-language learning, and theoretical predictions in a relevant psychology of second-language learning will be the surface structures of IL sentences.

By setting up these three sets of utterances within one theoretical framework, and by gathering as data utterances related to specific linguistic structures in each of these three systems, (under the *same* experimental conditions, if possible) the investigator in the psychology of second-language learning can begin to study the psycholinguistic processes which establish the knowledge which underlies IL behavior. I would like to suggest that there are five central processes (and perhaps some additional minor ones), and that they exist in the latent psychological structure referred to above. I consider the following to be processes *central* to second-language learning: first, *language transfer;* second, *transfer-of-training;* third, *strategies of second-language learning;* fourth, *strategies of second-language communication;* and fifth, *overgeneralization of TL linguistic material.* Each of the analyst's predictions as to the shape of IL utterances should be associated with one or more of these, or other, processes.

3.0 *Fossilization*

Before briefly describing these psycholinguistic processes, another notion I wish to introduce for the reader's consideration is the concept of *fossilization*, a mechanism which is assumed also to exist in the latent psychological structure described above. Fossilizable linguistic phenomena are linguistic items, rules, and subsystems which speakers of a particular NL will tend to keep in their IL relative to a particular TL, no matter what the age of the learner or amount of explanation and instruction he receives in the TL.[12] I have in mind such fossilizable structures as the well-known 'errors': French uvular /r/ in the English IL, American English retroflex /r/ in their French IL, English rhythm in the IL relative to Spanish, German *Time-Place* order after the verb in the English IL of German speakers, and so on. I also have in mind less well known 'non-errors' such as Spanish monophthong vowels in the IL of Spanish speakers relative to Hebrew, and Hebrew *Object-Time* surface order after the verb in the IL of Hebrew speakers relative to English. Finally, there are fossilizable structures that are much harder to classify such as some features of the Thai tone system in the IL of Thai speakers relative to English. It is important to note that fossilizable structures tend to remain as potential performance, reemerging[13] in the productive performance of an IL even when seemingly eradicated. Many of these phenomena reappear in IL performance when the learner's attention is focused upon new and difficult intellectual subject matter or when he is in a state of anxiety or other excitement, and strangely enough, sometimes when he is in a state of extreme relaxation. Note that the claim is made here that, whatever the cause, the well-observed phenomenon of 'backsliding' by second-language learners from a TL norm is not, as has been generally believed, either random or toward the speaker's NL, but toward an IL norm.[14]

A crucial fact, perhaps the most crucial fact, which any adequate theory of second-language learning will have to explain is this regular reappearance or reemergence in IL productive performance of linguistic structures which were thought to be eradicated. This behavioral reappearance is what has led me to postulate the reality of fossilization and ILs. It should be made clear that the reappearance of such behavior is not limited to the phonetic level. For example, some of the subtlest input information that a learner of a second language has to master regards subcategorization notions of verbal complementation. Indian English as an IL with regard to English[15] seems to fossilize the 'that complement' or *V that* construction for all verbs that take sentential complements. Even when the correct form has been learned by the Indian speaker of English, this type of knowledge is the first he seems to lose when his attention is diverted to new intellectual subject matter or when he has not spoken the TL for even a short time. Under conditions such as these, there is a regular reappearance of the 'that complement' in IL performance for all sentential complements.

4.0 *Five Central Processes*

It is my contention that the most interesting phenomena in IL performance are those items, rules, and subsystems which are fossilizable in terms of the five processes listed above. If it can be experimentally demonstrated that fossilizable items, rules, and subsystems which occur in IL performance are a result of the NL, then we are dealing with the process of *language transfer;* if these fossilizable items, rules, and subsystems are a result of identifiable items in training procedures, then we are dealing with the process known as the *transfer-of-training;* if they are a result of an identifiable approach by the learner to the material to be learned, then we are dealing with *strategies of second-language learning,* if they are a result of an identifiable approach by the learner to communication with native speakers of the TL, then we are dealing with *strategies of second-language communication;* and, finally, if they are a result of a clear overgeneralization of TL rules and semantic features, then we are dealing with the *overgeneralization of TL linguistic material.* I would like to hypothesize that these five processes are processes which are *central* to second-language learning, and that each process forces fossilizable material upon surface IL utterances, controlling to a very large extent the surface structures of these utterances.

Combinations of these processes produce what we might term entirely fossilized IL competences. Coulter (1968) presents convincing data to demonstrate not only *language transfer* but also a *strategy of communication* common to many second-language learners. This strategy of communications dictates to them, internally as it were, that they know enough of the TL in order to communicate. And they stop learning.[16] Whether they stop learning entirely or go on to learn in a minor way, e.g., adding vocabulary as experience demands [Jain (1969) insists they must] is, it seems to me, a moot point. If these individuals do not also learn the syntactic information that goes with lexical items, then adding a few new lexical items, say on space travel, is, I would argue, of little consequence. The important thing to note with regard to the evidence presented in Coulter (1968) and Jain (1969) is that not only can entire IL competences be fossilized in individual learners performing in their own interlingual situation,[17] but also in whole groups of individuals, resulting in the emergence of a new dialect (here Indian English), where fossilized IL competences may be the normal situation.

We will now provide examples of these processes. The examples presented in section 3 are almost certainly the result of the process of *language transfer*. A few examples relating to the other processes should suffice for this chapter.

4.1 *Overgeneralization of TL rules* is a phenomenon well-known to language teachers. Speakers of many languages could produce a sentence of the following kind in their English IL:

> (1) What did he intended to say?[18]

where the past tense morpheme -*ed* is extended to an environment in which, to the learner, it could logically apply, but just does not. The Indian speaker of English who produces the collocation *drive a bicycle* in his IL performance, as in (2):

> (2) After thinking little I decided to start on the *bicycle* as slowly as I could as it was not possible to *drive* fast.

is most probably overgeneralizing the use of *drive* to all vehicles (Jain, 1969, pp. 22 & 24; but see footnote 26 here). Most learners of English quickly learn the English rule of contraction which forms things like *the concert's* from *the concert is* but then these learners may overgeneralize this rule to produce sentences like:

> (3) Max is happier than Sam's these days.

in their English IL. Though this sentence is hypothetical, it illustrates an earlier point. The learner of English who produces contractions correctly in all environments must have learned the following constraint *without* 'explanation and instruction', since this constraint was discovered only recently: "contraction of auxiliaries. . .cannot occur when a constituent immediately following the auxiliary to be contracted has been deleted," e.g. 'happy' in (3) (Lakoff, in press). Dozens of examples of overgeneralization of TL rules are provided in Richards (1970).

4.2 The *transfer-of-training* is a process which is quite different from language transfer (see Selinker, 1969) and from overgeneralization of TL rules. It underlies the source of a difficulty which Serbo-Croatian speakers at all levels of English proficiency regularly have with the *he/she* distinction, producing in their English IL *he* on almost every occasion wherever *he* or *she* would be called for according to any norm of English. There is no language transfer effect here since, with regard to animateness, the distinction between *he* and *she* is the same in Serbo-Croation as it is in English.[19] According to a standard contrastive analysis then there should be no trouble. It seems to be the case that the resultant IL form, in the first instance, is due directly to the *transfer-of-training;* textbooks and teachers in this interlingual situation almost always present drills with *he* and never with *she.* The extent of this fossilization can be seen with respect to speakers of this IL over the age of 18, who even though they are consciously aware of the distinction and of their recurrent error, in fact, regularly produce *he* for both *he* and *she*, stating that they feel they do not need to make this distinction in order to communicate.[20] In this case, then, the fossilizable error is due originally to a type of *transfer-of-training* and later to a particular *strategy of second-language communication.*

4.3 Concerning the notion 'strategy' little is known in psychology about what constitutes a strategy; and a viable definition of it does not seem possible at present. Even less is known about strategies which learners of a second language use in their attempt to master a TL and express meanings in it. It has been pointed out[21] that learner strategies are probably culture-bound to some extent. For example, in many traditional cultures, chanting is used as a learning device, clearly relating to what is learned in these situations. Crucially, it has been argued[22] that strategies for handling TL material evolve whenever the learner realizes, either consciously or subconsciously, that he has no linguistic competence with regard to some aspect of the TL. It cannot be doubted that various internal strategies[23] on the part of the second-language learner affect to a large extent the surface structures of sentences underlying IL utterances. But exactly what these strategies might be and how they might work is at present pure conjecture. Thus, one can only roughly attribute the source of the examples presented herein to one or another strategy.

One example of a *strategy of second-language learning* that is widespread in many interlingual situations is a tendency on the part of learners to reduce the TL to a simpler system. According to Jain (1969, pp. 3 & 4), the results of this strategy are manifested at all levels of syntax in the IL of Indian speakers of English. For example, if the learner has adopted the strategy that all verbs are either transitive or intransitive, he may produce IL forms such as:

(4) I am feeling thirsty.

or

(5) Don't worry, I'm hearing him.

and in producing them seems to have adopted the further strategy that the realization of the category 'aspect' in its progressive form on the surface is always with -*ing* marking (for further discussion, see Jain, 1969, p. 3ff.).

Coulter (1968) reports systematic errors occurring in the English IL performance of two elderly Russian speakers of English, due to another strategy which seems also to be widespread in many interlingual situations: a tendency on the part of second-language learners to avoid grammatical formatives such as articles (6), plural forms (7), and past tense forms (8):

(6) It was ∅ nice, nice trailer, ∅ big one. (Coulter, 1968, p. 22)
(7) I have many hundred *carpenter* my own. (ibid, p. 29)
(8) I *was* in Frankfort when I *fill* application. (ibid, p. 36)

This tendency could be the result of a *learning strategy* of simplification, but Coulter (1968, p. 7 ff.) attributes it to a *communication strategy* due to the past experience of the speaker which has shown him that if he thinks about grammatical processes while attempting to express in English meanings which he already has, then his speech will be hesitant and disconnected, leading native speakers to be impatient with him. Also, Coulter claims that this *strategy of second-language communication* seemed to dictate to these speakers that a form such as the English plural "was not necessary for the kind of communicating they used" (ibid, p. 30).

Not all of these strategies, it must be pointed out, are conscious. A subconscious *strategy of second-language learning* called "cue-copying" has been experimented with by Crothers and Suppes (1967, p. 211) on Americans learning Russian morphological concepts. This "copy the cue" strategy is most probably due to what they call "probability matching", where the chance that the learner will select an alternative morphological ending related to the cue noun is not random. Crothers and Suppes do not provide examples of the result of this strategy in meaningful performance situations; an example would be the *r* at the end of words like *California* and *saw* which foreign students of English who have had teachers from the Boston area regularly reproduce in their English IL.

4.4 To conclude this section, it should be pointed out that beyond the five so-called *central* processes, there exist many other processes which account to some degree for the surface form of IL utterances. One might mention *spelling pronunciations*, e.g. speakers of many languages pronounce final -*er* on English words as [ε] plus some form of *r; cognate pronunciation,* e.g., English *athlete* pronounced as [atlit] by many Frenchmen whether or not they can produce [θ] in other English words;[24] *holophrase learning* (Jain, 1969), e.g. for *half-an-hour* the Indian learner of English may produce *one and half-an-hour; hypercorrection*, e.g. the Israeli who in attempting to get rid of his uvular fricative for English retroflex [r] produces [w] before front vowels, 'a vocalization too far forward';[25] and most assuredly others such as long exposure to signs and headlines which according to Jain (1969) affect by themselves the shape of English IL utterances of Indians, or at least reinforce more important processes such as *language transfer*.

5.0 *Problems with this perspective*

There are certainly many questions one might wish to ask regarding the perspective presented so far in this paper; I shall attempt to deal with five (5.1—5.5). The reader should bear in mind that we are here calling for the discovery, description and experimental testing of fossilizable items, rules and subsystems in interlanguages and the relating of these to the above-mentioned processes—especially to the central ones. What seems to be most promising for study is the observation concerning fossilization. Many IL linguistic structures are *never* really eradicated for most second-language learners; manifestations of these structures regularly reappear in IL productive performance, especially under conditions of anxiety, shifting attention, and second-language performance on subject matter which is new to the learner. It is this observation which allows us to claim that these psycholinguistic structures, even when seemingly eradicated, are still somehow present in the brain, stored by a fossilization mechanism (primarily through one of these five processes) in an IL. We further hypothesize that interlingual identifications uniting the three linguistic systems (NL, IL, and TL) psychologically, are activated in a latent psychological structure whenever an individual attempts to produce TL sentences.

5.1 The first problem we wish to deal with is: can we always unambiguously identify which of these processes our observable data is to be attributable to? Most probably not. It has been frequently pointed out (personal communication) that this situation is quite common in psychology. In studies on memory, for example, one often does not know whether one is in fact studying 'storage' or 'retrieval'. In our case, we may not know whether a particular constituent IL concatenation is a result of language transfer or of transfer-of-training or, perhaps, of both.[26] But this limitation need not deter us, even if we cannot always sort things out absolutely. By applying the constructs suggested in this paper, I believe that relevant data can be found in the very many second-language-learning situations around us.

5.2 The second problem is: how can we systematize the notion *fossilization* so that from the basis of theoretical constructs, we can predict which items in which interlingual situations will be fossilized? To illustrate the difficulty of attempting to answer this question, note in the following example the non-reversibility of fossilization effects for no apparent reason. According to a contrastive analysis, Spanish speakers should have no difficulty with the *he/she* distinction in English, nor should English speakers have any difficulty with the corresponding distinction in Spanish. The facts are quite different, however: Spanish speakers do, indeed, regularly have trouble with this distinction, while the reverse does not seem to occur with English learners of Spanish.[27] Unlike the Serbo-Croatian example mentioned above, in this case there is no clear-cut explanation why Spanish speakers have trouble and English speakers do not. In cases such as these, it may turn out that one process, e.g. language transfer or transfer-of-training, overrides other considerations, but the stating of the governing conditions may prove very difficult indeed.

In principle, one feels forced to agree with Stephanie Harries (personal communication) who claims that until a theory of second-language learning can answer questions like: "How do I recognize fossilizable structures in advance?" or "Why do some things fossilize and others do not?", all experiments conducted within the framework provided in this paper must be regarded as 'exploratory' in nature. (To put things in more familiar jargon: with regard to *fossilization,* our results are 'descriptive' and not 'explanatory' in nature.) But this task of prediction may prove to be impossible; certainly as Fred Lukoff points out (personal communication) this task, on the face of it, may be even tougher than trying to predict errors in second-language performance—a task notably lacking in success.

The major justification one has for writing about the construct 'fossilization' at this stage of knowledge is that descriptive knowledge about ILs which turns out to suggest predictions verifiable in meaningful performance situations, leads the way to a systematic collection of the relevant data; this task, one which is impossible without this construct, is expected to be relevant to serious theory construction in a psychology of second-language learning.

5.3 The third problem to be treated here concerns the apparent difficulty of fitting the following type of question into the idealized domain I have been sketching: how does a second-language-learning novice become able to produce IL utterances whose surface constituents are correct, i.e. 'correct' with respect to the TL whose norm he is attempting to produce? This question finally brings us face-to-face with the notion of 'success' in absolute terms: productive performance in the TL by the second-language learner which is identical to that produced by the native speaker of that TL.[28] We noted this in section 2 so as to exclude from our idealized domain of inquiry those learners of second languages who reactivate[29] the latent language structure that is realized into a native language. In this paper, we are concentrating on attempted learning of a second language, unsuccessful in this absolute sense. Of course, 'success' in second-language learning need not be defined so absolutely. The teacher or the learner can be satisfied with the learner's achieving what has been called 'communicative competence' (see, for example, Jakobovits, 1970, or Hymes, in press). But this is not the issue here. As was pointed out in section 1, the emphasis upon what the teacher has to do in order to help the learner achieve successful learning belongs to the 'teaching' perspective, which is not the perspective of this paper. Perhaps the rather curious confusion in the literature of 'learning a second language' with 'teaching a second language' (see footnote 2) can be explained by the failure to see a psychology of second-language learning in terms other than those related to 'success'. For example, typical learning-theory experiments when done in the domain of second-language learning would demand knowledge of where the learner will tend to end up, not where we would like him to end up. Experiments of this type would also demand knowledge of where the second-language learner begins. We would claim that prerequisite to both these types of knowledge are detailed descriptions of ILs—descriptions not presently available to us. Thus, such experiments at present are premature, with the results bound to prove confusing.

Specifically concerning the problem raised in the first sentence of 5.3, it seems to me that this question, though relevant to the psychology of second-language learning, is one that should also not be asked for the present since its asking depends upon our understanding clearly the psychological extent of interlingual identifications. For example, before we can discover how surface constituents in an IL get reorganized to identify with the TL, we must have a clear idea of what is in that IL, even if we cannot explain why it is there. In Selinker (1969) I believe I have shown that within a very limited interlingual situation, the basis from which linguistic material must be *reorganized* in order to be 'correct' has been operationally and unambiguously established. But I have there said nothing about the way in which successful learners do in fact reorganize linguistic material from this particular IL. Here we can speculate that as part of a definition of 'learning a second language', 'successful learning' of a second for most learners, involves, to a large extent, the *reorganization of linguistic material* from an IL to identity with a particular TL.

5.4 The fourth problem is: (a) what are the relevant units of this hypothesized latent psychological structure within which interlingual identifications exist and (b) is there any evidence for the existence of these units? If the relevant data of the psychology of second-language learning are in fact parallel utterances in three linguistic systems (NL, IL, and TL), then it seems to me reasonable to hypothesize that the only relevant, one might say, 'psychologically real', interlingual unit is one which can be described simultaneously for parallel data in the three systems, and, if possible, for experimentally-induced data in those systems.

Concerning underlying linguist structure, we should perhaps not be too surprised if it turns out not to matter whose model we need, if an eclectic one will do, or even if such notions as the 'cycle', 'tree pruning', or even 'derivation' prove not to have much relevance. If it is reasonable to assume that the only linguistically-relevant unit of a theory of second-language learning is one which is identified interlingually across three linguistic systems (NL, TL, and IL) by means of fossilization and the processes described in section 4, then it follows that no unit of linguistic theory, as these units are currently conceived, could fit this criterion. More generally, we should state that there is no necessary connection between relevant units of linguistic theory and linguistically-relevant units of a psychology of second-language learning.[30] That this assumption is obviously correct is clear to me; that many linguists will not be convinced is also clear.

For evidence of the relevant unit of surface syntactic structure, applying at one and the same time to these three linguistic systems, I refer the reader to experimental evidence appearing in my paper on language transfer (Selinker, 1969). In those experiments subjects responded orally in their native language to questions presented orally in their NL and attempted to respond in English to parallel questions presented in English. The questions came from an interview designed to elicit manifestations of specific types of surface structures in certain syntactic domains. The only experimental instruction given was for each subject to speak in a 'complete sentence'. Replicated results showed that the interlingual unit of surface syntactic structure transferred from NL to IL (*not* to TL) was a unit roughly equivalent to the traditional direct object or to an adverb of place, an adverb of time, an adverb of degree, and so on. I would claim that this unit, a surface constituent labelled the *syntactic string*, has a behavioral unity both in the experimental situation and in meaningful performance situations,[31] and thus, if the results were replicated in other 'interlingual situations' (i.e. other combinations of NL, TL, and IL), would account for a large class of IL events.

With regard to a 'realizational unit', i.e., a syntactic string tied to a specific semantic notion, replicated results from this same series of experiments show that responses concerning a topic such as 'subjects studied in school', as opposed to other topics such as 'buying and receiving things' and 'seeing movies and parades', affected very drastically the surface concatenation of the above-mentioned strings.[32] This semantic effect on surface syntactic order in an interlingual study, if further replicated in other interlingual situations, would provide very powerful evidence for the transfer of the whole realizational unit as well as for its candidacy as the unit of realizational structure in interlingual identifications.

Concerning the notion of relevant units on the phonological level, it seems to me that Brière (1968) has demonstrated that for his data there are several relevant units. The relevant units do not always correspond to known linguistic units, but rather would depend on the sounds involved; sometimes the taxonomic phoneme is the unit, but the unit in other cases seems not to be describable in purely linguistic terms. Brière evolved an experimental technique which imitated to a large extent actual methods of teaching advocated by applied structural linguists: listening to TL sounds, attempted imitation, use of phonemic transcription, physiological explanations, and so on. If I may be allowed to reinterpret Brière's data, it seems to me that he has been working, in another interlingual situation, with exactly the three systems we are discussing here, NL, TL, and IL: first, NL utterances which were hypothesized utterances in American English; second, TL utterances which were actual utterances in the 'composite language' Brière set up, each utterance having been produced by a native speaker of French, Arabic, or Vietnamese; third, IL utterances which were actual utterances produced by native speakers of this NL when attempting to produce this particular TL norm. Regarding the sounds /ž/ and /ŋ/ in his TL corpus, the unit identified interlingually across these three systems is the taxonomic phoneme defined distributionally within the syllable as opposed to within the word (Brière, 1968, p. 73). For other sounds the relevant phonological unit of interlingual identifications is not the taxonomic phoneme, but may be based on phonetic parameters some of which, he says, are probably not known (ibid., pp. 64 & 73).

If these units in the domain of interlingual identifications are not necessarily the same units as those in the native-speaker domain, then where do they come from? An interesting bit of speculation about native-speaker performance units is provided by Haggard (1967, p. 335) who states that searching for "*the* unit" in native-speaker speech-perception is a waste of time. Alternative units may be available to native-speakers, for example under noise conditions.[33] While other explanations are surely possible for the well-known fact that noise conditions affect performance in a second language, and sometimes drastically, we can not ignore the possible relevance of Haggard's intriguing suggestion: That alternative language units are available to individuals and that these units are activated under certain conditions. It fits in very well with the perspective outlined in this chapter to postulate a new type of psycholinguistic unit, available to an individual whenever he attempts to produce sentences in a second language. This interlingual unit stretches, we hypothesize, across three linguistic systems: NL, IL, and TL, and becomes available to the idealized second-language learner who will not achieve native-speaker competence in the TL, whenever he attempts to express meanings, which he may already have, in a TL he is learning, i.e., whenever he attempts to produce a TL norm. These units become available to the learner only after he has switched his psychic set or state from the native-speaker domain to the new domain of interlingual identifications. I would like to postulate further that these relevant units of interlingual identifications do not come from anywhere; they are latent in the brain in a latent psychological structure, available to an individual whenever he wishes to attempt to produce the norm of any TL.

5.5 The final difficulty with this perspective which we will treat here is the following: how can we experiment with three linguistic systems, creating the same experimental conditions for each, with one unit which is identified interlingually across these systems? I can only refer the reader once again to my own experiments on language transfer (Selinker, 1969) where manifestations of desired concatenations of particular surface syntactic structures were obtained in what, I believe, was an efficient and valid manner. An oral interview technique was used; the purpose of the interview was to achieve a similar framework in the three systems which served the interviewer as a guide in his attempt to elicit certain types of sentences from the subjects. Upon request, I am prepared to make available a transcript of this interview as well as some thoughts for its improvement. Future experimental work, to be undertaken within this perspective, will go toward investigating the kind and extent of linguistic structures amenable to this particular technique.

6.0 *Summary*

The following are some assumptions which are necessary for research into the linguistic aspects of the psychology of second-language learning and which have been suggested by the above discussion.

1) In a theory of second-language learning, those behavioral events which are to be counted as relevant data are not immediately obvious.

2) These data have to be organized with the help of certain theoretical constructs.

3) Some theoretical constructs relevant to the way in which 'adults' actually learn second languages are: interlingual identifications, native language (NL), target language (TL), interlanguage (IL), fossilization, syntactic string, taxonomic phoneme, phonetic feature.

4) The psychologically-relevant data of second-language learning are utterances in TL by native speakers, and in NL and IL by second-language learners.

5) Interlingual identifications by second-language learners is what unites the three linguistic systems (NL, TL, and IL) psychologically. These learners focus upon one norm of the TL.

6) Theoretical predictions in a relevant psychology of second-language learning must be the surface structures of IL sentences.

7) Successful second-language learning, for most learners, is the reorganization of linguistic material from an IL to identity with a particular TL.

8) There exist five distinct processes which are central to second-language learning: language transfer, transfer-of-training,

strategies of second-language learning, strategies of second-language communication, and overgeneralization of TL linguistic material.

9) Each prediction in (6) should be made, if possible, relative to one of the five processes in (8).

10) There is *no* necessary connection between relevant units of linguistic theory and linguistically-relevant units of a psychology of second-language learning.

11) The only linguistically-relevant unit of a psychology of second-language learning is one which is identified interlingually across the three linguistic systems: NL, TL, and IL.

12) The *syntactic string* is the unit of surface structure transfer and part of the unit of realizational transfer.

13) The *taxonomic phoneme* is, in the case of some sounds, the unit of interlingual phonology, while in other cases no purely linguistic unit seems relevant.

14) There exists a *latent psychological structure*, i.e., an already formulated arrangement in the brain, which is activated whenever an adult attempts to produce meanings, which he may have, in a second language which he is learning.

15) Interlingual identifications, the units mentioned in (12) and (13), and the processes listed in (8) exist in this latent psychological structure.

16) *Fossilization,* a mechanism which also exists in this latent psychological structure, underlies surface linguistic material which speakers will tend to keep in their IL productive performance, no matter what the age of the learner or the amount of instruction he receives in the TL.

17) The fossilization mechanism accounts for the phenomenon of the regular reappearance in IL productive performance of linguistic material which was thought to be eradicated.

18) This latent psychological structure, for most learners, is different from and exists in addition to the *latent language structure* described by Lenneberg (1967, pp. 374—379).

19) These two latent structures differ in the following ways: (a) the latent psychological structure has no genetic time-table; (b) it has no direct counterpart to any grammatical concept; (c) it may not be activated at all; (d) it may never be realized into a natural language; and (e) it may overlap with other intellectual structures.

20) The qualification ('for most learners') in (7) and (18) is necessary, since those adults who seem to achieve native-speaker 'competence', i.e. those who learn a second language so that their 'performance' is indistinguishable from that of native speakers

(perhaps a mere 5% of all learners), have not been taught this performance through 'explanation and instruction' but have somehow reactivated this latent language structure.

21) Since it is assumed that the two structures mentioned in (18) are different and since we know very little about the latent language structure and its activation, then the 5% mentioned in (20) should be ignored in setting up the idealizations which guide us to the psychologically-relevant data of second-language learning.

Reprinted from *IRAL*, Vol. 10, No. 3, by permission of the author and publishers.

FOOTNOTES

[1]This chapter was begun during the 1968-69 academic year while I was a visitor at the Dept. of Applied Linguistics, University of Edinburgh. Many students and teachers at Edinburgh and at Washington, through their persistent calls for clarity, have helped me to crystallize the ideas presented in this chapter to whatever level of clarity is attained herein. I wish to thank them and I especially wish to thank Ruth Clark, Fred Lukoff, Frederick Newmeyer, and Paul Van Buren. An earlier version of this chapter was given as a paper at the Second International Congress of Applied Linguistics, Cambridge University, Sept., 1969.

[2]It is not unfair to say that almost all of the vast literature attempting to relate psycholinguistics to second-language learning, whether produced by linguists or psychologists, is characterized by confusion between 'learning' a second language and 'teaching' a second language. (See also Mackey in Jakobovits, 1970, p. IX.) This confusion applies as well to almost all discussions on the topic one hears. For example, one might hear the term 'psychology of second-language teaching' and not know whether the speaker is referring to what the teacher should do, what the learner should do, or both. This terminological confusion makes one regularly uncertain as to what is being claimed.

[3]The answer to this question is not obvious since it is well known that theoretical considerations help point the way to relevant data. See, for example, Fodor (1968, p. 48): ". . .how we count behaviors and what is available as a description depends in part on what conceptual equipment our theories provide. . ."

[4]'Adult' is defined as being over the age of 12. This notion is derived from Lenneberg (1967), e.g., pp. 156, 176) who claims that after the onset of puberty, it is difficult to master the pronunciation of a second language since a "critical" period in brain maturation has been passed, and ". . .language development tends to 'freeze' " (ibid, 156).

[5]First pointed out by Harold Edwards.

[6]See Lawler and Selinker (forthcoming) where the relevance of counterfactuals to a theory of second-language learning is taken up.

[7]Chomsky (1969, p. 68) expresses a very similar view:
". . .it must be recognized that one does not learn the grammatical structure of a second language through 'explanation and instruction', beyond the most elementary rudiments, for the simple reason that no one has enough explicit knowledge about this structure to provide explanation and instruction." Chomsky gives as a detailed example a property which is clearly central to grammar: that of nominalization (Chomsky, 1969, pp. 68 and 52-60). I see no point in repeating Chomsky's detailed arguments which clearly show that a successful learner of English as a second language could not have learned to make the judgments Chomsky describes through 'explanation and instruction'.

[8]We have also idealized out of our consideration differences between individual learners, which makes this framework quite incomplete. A theory of second-language learning that does not provide a central place for individual differences among learners *cannot* be considered acceptable. See Lawler and Selinker (forthcoming) for a discussion of this tricky question in terms of profiles of idealized learners who differ one from the other with respect to types of linguistic rules and types of meaningful performance in a second language.

[9]There has been a great deal of misunderstanding (personal communication) of this point. I am not taking an antimentalist position here. Neither am I ruling out on an a-priori basis perceptual studies in a second language. However, the reader should be aware that in addition to the usual problems with determining whether a subject perceives or understands an utterance, the analyst in the interlingual domain cannot rely on intuitive grammatical judgments since he will gain information about another system, the one the learner is struggling with, i.e., the TL. (For a similar methodological problem in another domain, see Labov, 1969, p. 715). Another, and perhaps the most important, argument against perceptual interlingual studies is that predictions based upon them are not testable in 'meaningful performance situations' (see definition above); a reconstruction of the event upon the part of the learner would have to be made in a perceptual interlingual study. Such difficulties do not exist when predictions are related to the shape of utterances produced as the result of the learner attempting to express in the TL meanings which he may already have.

[10]Notions of such separate linguistic systems have been developed independently by Jakobovits (1969) and Nemser (1971).

[11]The notion 'interlanguage' is introduced in Selinker (1969).

[12]Gillian Brown has pointed out (personal communication) that we should work here towards a dynamic model where fossilization would be defined relative to various, perhaps arbitrary, chronological age groups.

[13]John Laver has helped me to clarify this point.

[14]Several people have pointed out (personal communication) that, in this paragraph, there appears to be a connection solely between fossilization and errors. This connection is not intended since it turns out that 'correct' things can also reemerge when thought to be eradicated, especially if they are caused by processes other than language transfer.

[15]Keith Brown (personal communication) has argued that the sociolinguistic status of the 'languages' or 'dialects' called Indian English, Filipino English, West African English, West African French, and so on, places them in a different category from that of the IL situation which I have been describing. From the sociolinguistic point of view this argument might be justified, but I am concerned in this chapter with a psychological perspective and the relevant idealizations seem to me to be identical in all of these cases.

[16]To describe this situation, Jain (1969) speaks of *functional competence.* Corder (1967) using the term *transitional competence* focuses on the provisional aspect of developing

'competence' in a second language. Both these notions owe their existence in the first place, to Chomsky's (1965) notion of linguistic competence which is to be distinguished from actual linguistic performance.

[17] An 'interlingual situation' is defined as a specific combination of NL, TL, and IL.

[18] This sentence and sentences like it were in fact produced consistently by a middle-aged Israeli who was *very* fluent in English.

[19] I am indebted to Wayles Browne (personal communication) for clarification of this point.

[20] Reported by George McCready (personal communication).

[21] Ian Pearson (personal communication).

[22] Elaine Tarone (personal communication).

[23] That is, what Corder refers to as the learner's "built-in syllabus" (Corder, 1967).

[24] Example from Tom Huckin (personal communication).

[25] Example from Briana Stateman (personal communication).

[26] The *drive a bicycle* example given in section 4 may, in fact, fit this situation (see Jain, 1969, p. 24).

[27] Example from Sol Saporta (personal communication).

[28] As was pointed out in footnote 7, Chomsky (1969, p. 68) also adds the ability to provide native-speaker-like grammaticality judgments.

[29] Note that this reactivation may be the only explanation possible for an individual who learns *any* part of a second language well. In this light, Cheryl Goodenough (personal communication) has objected to the qualitative split between the 5% who succeed and the rest of all second-language learners. Since in this chapter we are not concentrating on success in a second language, as one would in the teaching approach, but on the attempt to isolate the latent psychological structure which determines, for any learner, the system underlying attempted production of a TL norm where the total effect of this output is clearly non-identity to the hypothesized TL norm, then resolution of this issue should not affect the discussion. The importance of isolating this 5% is the speculation that these individuals may not go through an IL.
Reibel (1969) stresses the role of the latent language structure in second-language learning by suggesting that it is only when second-language learners do the wrong things that they do not "succeed," i.e., "we seek to explain differences between adult learners, not in terms of differences in the innate learning abilities, but rather in terms of the way in which they are applied." (p. 8) Kline (1970) attempts to provide a point of contact between Reibel's views and mine by suggesting that any reorganization of an IL to identity with a TL must use the kinds of capacities and abilities Reibel describes.
A different opposing view to the perspective of this chapter has been presented by Sandra Hamlett and Michael Seitz (personal communication) who have argued that, even for the vast majority of second-language learners, there is no already formulated arrangement existing in the brain, but that the latent psychological structure alluded to here is developed, partly at least, by strategies which change up to the age of 12 and remain with an individual for the rest of his life. There seems to be at present no critical empirical test for deciding between these two alternatives.

[30] It is important to bear in mind that we are here working in the domain of 'interlingual identifications' and thus are in a different counterfactual domain (Lawler and Selinker, forthcoming) than linguists who work in the domain of the "ideal speaker-listener" (Chomsky, 1965). It seems to me that researchers in the psychology of second-language

learning are in the analogous position to the language teacher who, Chomsky (1966) admonishes, has the burden of deciding what in linguistics and psychology is relevant to his needs.
Nevertheless, the linguistic status of ILs has still to be determined. One would like to know, for example, whether such things as transformations occur in IL grammars. Watkin (1970) asks whether the rules of IL are of the same general construction or shape as the rules for the same phenomena in the second language, "or are they in a 'recoded' form?" Watkin's data implies the same type of fossilization related to some similarity among rules of different ILs.

[31]The surface domain considered was constituent concatenation after the verb. Sample results showed statistically-significant parallel trends for NL (Hebrew) and IL (English) *Object and Time* constituents on the one hand and (direct) *Object and Adverb* (of degree) on the other. That is, whenever an *Object* constituent and a *Time* constituent occurred after the verb, the statistically-dominant surface order was *Object-Time*, and not the reverse, both concerning NL responses, e.g., (9), and IL responses, e.g. (10):
(9) raiti [et haseret haze] [lifney švuaim]
'I saw that movie two weeks ago'
(10) I met [Mrs. Cosman] [today]
But whenever an *Object* constituent and an *Adverb* constituent occurred after the verb, the statiscally-dominant surface order was *Adverb-Object*, and not the reverse, both concerning NL responses, e.g., (11) and IL responses, e.g., (12):
(11) ani ohev [meod] [stratim] 'I like movies very much'
(12) I like [very much] [movies]
Importantly, these and all other experimental results were controlled informally by observing speakers of all ages over 12, from this interlingual situation, producing IL utterances in meaningful performance situations.

[32]That is, when the responses concerned the topic 'subjects studied at school', there occurred an almost absolute trend toward both the NL (Hebrew) order *Place-Object* noun after the verb, e.g., (13), and toward the same IL (English) order of surface constituents, e.g., (14):
(13) ani roca lilmod [bauniversita] [biologia]
'I want to study biology at the university'
(14) I will study [in the university] [biology]
But when the responses concerned other topics such as the other two topics mentioned in the text, there occurred an almost absolute trend toward both the NL order *Object* noun *Place* after the verb, e.g., (15) and toward the same IL order of surface constituents, e.g., (16):
(15) kaniti [et hašaon] [baxanut]
'I bought the watch in the store'
(16) I bought [my watch] [in Tel Aviv]
For further details, see Selinker (1969) sections 3.41 and 3.42.

[33]The fact that Haggard is concerned with alternative units which are inclusive in larger units has no bearing on the issue under discussion in this section.

REFERENCES

Brière, Eugène J.: *A Psycholinguistic Study of Phonological Interference.* Mouton, 1968.

Chomsky, Noam: *Aspects of the Theory of Syntax.* M.I.T. Press, 1965.

Chomsky, Noam: "Linguistic Theory", *Northeast Conference on the Teaching of Foreign Languages*, 43-49, 1966.

Chomsky, Noam: "Linguistics and Philosophy", in *Language and Philosophy*, ed. by Sidney Hook, New York University Press, 1969, 51-94.

Corder, S. Pit: "The Significance of Learner's Errors", *IRAL*, 5 (1967), 161-170.

Coulter, Kenneth: "Linguistic Error-Analysis of the Spoken English of Two Native Russians." Unpublished M. A. thesis, University of Washington, 1968.

Crothers, Edward and Suppes, Patrick: *Experiments in Second-Language Learning*. Academic Press, 1967.

Fodor, Jerry A.: *Psychological Explanation: An Introduction to the Philosophy of Psychology*. Random House, 1968.

Haggard, Mark P.: "Models and Data in Speech Perception", in *Models for the Perception of Speech and Visual Form*, ed. by Weiant Wathen-Dunn, M.I.T. Press, 1967, 331-339.

Hymes, Dell: *On Communicative Competence*. Penguin, (in press).

Jain, Mahavir: "Error Analysis of an Indian English Corpus." Unpublished paper, University of Edinburgh, 1969.

Jakobovits, Leon A.: "Second Language Learning and Transfer Theory: a Theoretical Assessment", *Language Learning*, 19 (June, 1969(, 55-86.

Jakobotivs, Leon A.: *Foreign Language Learning: A Psycholinguistic Analysis of the Issues*. Newbury House, 1970.

Kline, Helen: "Research in the Psychology of Second-Language Learning." Unpublished paper, University of Minnesota, 1970.

Labov, William: "Contraction, Deletion, and Inherent Variability of the English Copula", *Language*, 45.4 (1969), 715-762.

Lakoff, George: "On Generative Semantics", in *Semantics–An Interdisciplinary Reader in Philosophy, Linguistics, Anthropology and Psychology*, ed. by Danny Steinberg and Leon Jakobovits. Cambridge University Press, (in press).

Lawler, John and Selinker, Larry: "On Paradoxes, Rules, and Research in Second-Language Learning", *Language Learning* (in press).

Lenneberg, Eric H.: *Biological Foundations of Language*. John Wiley and Sons Inc., 1967.

Nemser, William: "Approximative Systems of Foreign Language Learners", *IRAL* 9 (1971), 115-123.

Reibel, D.A.: "Language Learning Strategies for the Adult", paper read at *Second International Congress of Applied Linguistics*, Cambridge University, Sept., 1969.

Richards, Jack C.: "A Non-Contrastive Approach to Error Analysis." Paper delivered at TESOL Convention, San Francisco, March, 1970.

Selinker, Larry: "Language Transfer", *General Linguistics*, 9 (1969), 67-92.

Watkin, K. L.: "Fossilization and Its Implications Regarding the Interlanguage Hypothesis." Unpublished paper, University of Washington, 1970.

Weinreich, Uriel: *Languages in Contact*. The Linguistic Circle of New York, 1953.

k.

IMPLICATIONS OF PIDGINIZATION AND CREOLIZATION FOR THE STUDY OF ADULT SECOND LANGUAGE ACQUISITION

JOHN H. SCHUMANN

1.0 *Pidginization and Creolization*

A pidgin is a language that develops to meet the communication needs of two or more groups of people who speak different languages and who are in a contact situation. A typical example is that of traders (generally of European origin) speaking language X who come in contact with a group of people (usually indigenous natives of non-European origin) speaking language Y. In order to communicate, a pidgin (language Z) develops. This pidgin is a second language of both parties and is used simply as an auxiliary vehicle of communication. The intrusion of a third group who speak language A and who then learn the pidgin tends to make the pidgin stabilize. A creole evolves when speakers of languages X and Y intermarry and the pidgin becomes the first language of their children.

1.1 *The Origin of Pidgins*

There are both monogenetic and polygenetic theories of the origin of pidgins. The monogenetic theory holds that a single language such as the Portuguese version of the famous Lingua Franca of the Mediterranean, Sabir, was the source of all European-based pidgins and creoles. This proto-pidgin is thought to be as old as the crusades. Within the monogenetic theory, similarities among various pidgins and creoles are accounted for by the fact that all existing pidgins are seen as relexifications of this original Portuguese pidgin. In other words, the grammatical structure of the original pidgin has been largely maintained but its vocabulary has changed under the influences of other languages. Thus English, French and Spanish based pidgins and creoles would merely be relexifications of the original proto-pidgin. (Decamp, 1971, pp. 22-23)

Polygenesis has several versions. The earliest version, expounded by Hall (1966, p. 86), holds that pidgins began when masters, plantation owners, merchants and sailors attempted to imitate the natives' attempts to reproduce the foreigners' speech. For example, the natives would reduce and simplify English when they attempted to communicate with Englishmen. The Englishmen in turn would use a spontaneously reduced form of their language when responding to and addressing the natives. There is some belief that a systematic process of simplification and reduction operates both when the speakers of a language communicate with people who are attempting to learn it (Ferguson, 1971) and by learners when attempting to communicate with native speakers of a different language (Smith 1971, p. 15).

Whinnom (1971) takes another point of view. He distinguishes between primary, secondary and tertiary hybridization. Primary hybridization is the breaking up of a species-language into dialects. Secondary hybridization is exemplified by the interlanguage spoken by a second language learner. In some situations this interlanguage is continually renewed by new learners and thus becomes a recognizable variety of speech. The *cocoliche* once spoken by Italian immigrants to Argentina is an example of this stage of hybridization. *Cocoliche* was completely unstable in individuals because as the learner became more proficient, his interlanguage continually evolved in the direction of Spanish. In addition, the *cocoliche* of not two individuals was exactly the same. Each contained different lexical and grammatical features depending on which of these features the individual speaker had been exposed to in standard Spanish. Nevertheless, this interlanguage remained a predictable, systematic and recognizable speech form from generation to generation of Italian immigrants.

Tertiary hybridization, which Whinnom considers necessary for the development of a true pidgin, arises when the target language is removed from consideration. Thus *cocoliche* might have become a pidgin in the Whinnom sense if the Italian immigrants had, at some time, been cut off or isolated from Spanish speakers. In a similar vein, the interlanguage spoken by an English-speaking student while attempting to communicate in French with a French-speaking student would not be considered a pidgin. However, the interlanguage used by an English-speaking student and a German-speaking student when trying to communicate with each other in French would qualify as a pidgin. This is assuming that in the latter case both speakers are deprived of a French model upon which they could improve their performance and also that both speakers lack the motivation to improve it. Thus for Whinnom, one essential element in the development of a pidgin is the absence of or distance from the target language norm. Whinnom also holds that a pidgin is primarily a vehicle of communication between groups of people who do not speak the base language. Thus, he would claim that Chinese Pidgin English is used more for intercommunication among speakers of different Chinese dialects, than between speakers of Chinese and speakers of English.

In contrast to Whinnom, writers such as Samarin and Hall see the process of pidginization as a much more widespread phenomenon. Both would accept the interlanguage of second language learners (secondary hybridization) as legitimate pidginization.

Decamp (1971, p. 20) quotes Hall on this issue:

> A pidgin normally owes its origin to relatively casual, short-term contact between groups which do not have a language in common... a pidgin can arise—on occasion, even in the space of only a few hours—whenever an emergency calls for communication on a minimal level of comprehension.

Hymes (1971, p. 69) describes Samarin's position:

> ... but whereas imperfect learning of a second language is set aside by Whinnom, for Samarin, it, memory loss of one's language, field work jargons, argots, restricted codes (Bernstein), and the like are all of interest, inasmuch as they are instances, not of pidgins necessarily, but of a process of pidginization, which he defines as any consistent reduction of the functioning of a language both in its grammar and its use.

It is generally accepted that there is a prepidgin—post creole continuum on which we may find prepidgin forms, crystalized pidgins, pidgins undergoing depidginization (reabsorption by its dominant source), pidgins undergoing creolization, creoles and creoles undergoing decreolization. (Hymes 1971, p. 78) The variety of polygenesis that will serve, in this paper, as the basis for speculation about second language acquisition will include prepidgin forms (secondary hybridization, learner language), crystalized pidgins and pidgins undergoing creolization. Crystalized pidgins, according to the above formulation, are generally maintained at a distance from the target language norm, and therefore perhaps do not reflect second language learning situations quite as well as prepidgins. Nevertheless, since their function (as will be seen below) corresponds very closely to the function of learner language in the early stages of second language acquisition, they, in addition to prepidgins and incipient creoles, offer highly probable predictions about what forms will appear in the interlanguage of second language learners.

1.2 *Simplification and Reduction*

David Smith (1971) has analyzed the function of language into three components: communicative, integrative and expressive.

Through the communicative function information is exchanged among persons. The integrative function serves to mark one's identity within society and the expressive function is designed to allow the expression of certain psychological needs. Pidgin languages are generally restricted to the first function — communication. That is, their purpose is merely to convey information. Since pidgins are always second languages, the integrative and expressive functions are maintained by the speakers' native languages. As a result of this functional restriction, pidginization produces an interlanguage which is simplified in outer form and reduced in inner form. The simplification process yields several salient characteristics which are illustrated below by David Smith in examples taken from both West African Pidgin English (WAPE) and Neo-Melanesian.

1. Word order tends to replace inflectional morphology. This can be illustrated by a verb paradigm from WAPE.

i cop	He eats, is eating, etc. (unmarked)
i bin cop	He eats
i don cop	He has eaten
i de cop	He is, was, will be eating
i go cop	He will eat
i bin de cop	He was eating
i bin don cop	He had eaten
i go don cop	He will have eaten
i go de cop	He will be eating
i wan cop	He wants to eat
i get fo cop	He should eat (Smith, p. 9)

English, like many natural languages, often uses both word order and morphological inflection in grammatical constructions. This combination produces language which is redundant. For example, in the sentence *He eats*, both *he* and the ending -*s* indicate third person singular. In the construction *five books*, the number *five* and the ending -*s* indicate plurality. "This redundancy is one of the things which makes language useful in performing integrative and expressive functions." (Smith, p. 9) However, since pidgins are used only for communication these redundant features become unnecessary.

2. Certain grammatical transformations tend to be eliminated in pidginization.

   a. Pidgins usually lack agnate sentences such as active-passive constructions. Smith offers these examples from Neo-Melanesian: In English we can say *He often buys books.* or *Books are often bought by him.* In Neo-Melanesian there is only one form, *Oltaim em i baiim sampela buk.* The active sentence in English *John gave him two books.* has two passive forms, *He was given two books by John.* and *Two books were given him by John.* In Neo-Melanesian there is only one form, *Jan i bin givim em tupela buk.* (Smith, pp. 11—12) The elimination of such stylistic devices again reflects the restriction to the communicative function.

b. The reduction in grammatical transformations can also be illustrated by comparing the word order combinations in English and Neo-Melanesian questions.

English:

I / am building / a house.	(1 2 3)
Who / is building / a house?	(1 2 3)
Are / you / building / a house?	(2 1 2 3)
What / are / you / building?	(3 2 1 2)
What / are / you / doing?	(3 2 1 2)

Neo-Melanesian:

Mi / wokim / haus.	(1 2 3)
Husat / i wokim / haus?	(1 2 3)
Yu / wokim / haus?	(1 2 3)
Yu / mekim / wanem samting?	(1 2 3)
Yu / mekim / wanem?	(1 2 3) (Smith, p. 12)

These paradigms show that whereas the English questions vary in their surface structure, Neo-Melanesian interrogatives all maintain the same word order and that order is identical to the statement form. Thus, a question transformation is virtually absent in Neo-Melanesian.

c. The reduction in grammatical transformations also makes the surface structures of pidgins more closely resemble their deep structures. Traugott (1972, p. 44)[1] quotes Kay and Sankoff (1972) on this point,

> "pidgin languages are derivationally shallower than natural . . . languages and reflect universal deep (=semantic) structure in their surface structures more directly than do natural languages"

> For example, the verb in *He arranged it*, in English could be analyzed semantically as comprising several discrete actions. In pidgin this sentence would be rendered, *i bin tek am muf am put am fo da ples.* (Lit.,"He took it, moved it, and put it someplace else.") What in English is only analyzable at an underlying level is realized on the surface in West African Pidgin English. (Smith, p. 16)

Bever and Langendoen (1971, p. 49) claim that disappearance of inflections makes a language easier to learn, but that the language then becomes more difficult to understand because it no longer has the surface cues (inflections) to the underlying structure. From this point of view it would appear that the underlying structures of pidgins are less accessible than those of their base languages. However, there are devices used in some pidgins that may serve to get around just this point and to keep deep structure relations evident in the surface structures. Neo-Melanesian has a predicate marker /i/ which marks the major constituent boundary within a clause.

jumi tufela i-go — the two of us go (Leachman and Hall 1955, p. 170)

disfela haws i-bigfela — this house is big (Leachman and Hall 1955, p. 170)

najf disfela mastər i-givim loŋ mi — knife (which) the man gave to me (Hall 1966, p. 71)

Neo-Melanesian also has a transitive verb suffic /əm/ which marks the constituent break within the verb phrase (i.e., between V and the following NP):

mi lukəm ju   I see you

American Indian Pidgin English which is discussed below also has these devices.

3. Pidgins tend to have a radically reduced lexicon.

a. Whereas most normal languages are characterized by words having the same denotata but different connotata, pidgin words have few connotations. For example, in English *house* and *home* both denote the same thing—*dwelling*. However, their connotations are different. *House* usually means a building which serves as living quarters; *home* can also mean a family's place of residence and/or the social unit formed by that family. With the reduction in connotata resulting from pidginization both *house* and *home* would only have one meaning, that of *dwelling*. Therefore the two words would be seen as redundant and one form would not be used.

b. Pidgins also tend to delete monomorphic words such as "calf" and "puppy" and instead use two-word substitutes, one indicating the larger category and the other indicating "young." Thus in West African Pidgin English calf and puppy would be rendered *kaw pikin*, "baby cow" and *dok pikin*, "baby dog." (Smith, pp. 10-11)

John Goodman (1967) has described the development of an English-Japanese Pidgin which appeared in Hamamatsu in the mid 1950's. His report is particularly interesting because it deals with a case of pidginization which closely resembles a second language acquisition situation. The pidgin was recorded at its very early stages of development when it only had a minimum of established conventions, thus it represents early pidginization of the pre-pidgin variety. Pidgins are often thought of as developing in situations where one of the languages involved is spoken by a socially or economically dominant group and the other language or languages by a substrata group. This is not the case with the English-Japanese Pidgin. No clear dominance pattern emerged in its development; during the period it was observed it appeared to remain a mixture of both languages. (pp. 43-44)

The pidgin was created when United States Air Force advisors were assigned to work with Japanese counterparts in several training programs in Hamamatsu. Very friendly relations existed between both groups; a good deal of effort was made to keep these relations cordial.

> The basic attitude on both sides was one of essential friendliness and curiosity. Haphazardly diffused cultural items were received with delight. The Americans enjoyed sorobans, flower-arrangements, and sake; the Japanese enjoyed shaving lotion, chewing gum, and canned soft drinks. (p. 46)

The amazing mutual intelligibility of the pidgin was fostered not only by the pidgin as a language, but also by gestures, voice changes, facial expressions and "a social atmosphere of amused friendliness." (p. 44) Goodman has categorized these gestures. Smiles indicated good will in situations of social uncertainty. A giggle showed embarrassment, astonishment or indecision. A touch or slap on the shoulder was used to give reassurance. (p. 48)

The E J-Pidgin contained common morphosyntactic patterns and lexicon but differed in phonology. The American when speaking pidgin used English phones and sometimes altered them slightly in the direction of what he considered to be Japanese. The Japanese speaker employed the pidgin in the same way. Thus each speaker generally used the phones of his own language but was able to recognize the diaphonic correspondences in the speech of the other. (p. 44 and p. 50).

The grammar of E J-Pidgin had the following characteristics:
1. Reduplication of forms:
   testo-testo — to examine, an analysis
   meter-meter — to look over, an examination
   saymo-saymo — similar, alike
   hubba-hubba — to hurry
   dammey-dammey — not good. (p. 51)

Hymes (1971, p. 72) states such reduplication is characteristic of English-based pidgins perhaps because English speakers put it there. He also suggests that it might be a reflection of what Americans consider to be simple.

2. Absence of tense markers, definite article and copula. Adverbs were used instead of tense to indicate time: [ašta] from Japanese /ašita/ was used for *tomorrow*, [kino] from Japanese /kino/ indicated *yesterday*. These adverbs were almost always accompanied by either backward or forward hand motions. The verb forms from both languages appeared in either their infinitive or citation forms without inflectional affixes. (p. 52)

3. The major syntactic pattern was the use of juxtaposition of terms in topic-comment order. Goodman offers the following example:

> The American, seeing a Japanese male cook leave the small restaurant with one of the Japanese waitresses said: Sayonara. Meter-meter dai jobu; testo-testo dammey-dammey. The rough gloss is: sayonara *good bye*; dai jobu *OK, very good*; testo-testo *tryout, examine*; dammey-dammey *no good*. In the specific context of friendliness between the American and the Japanese cook and with the accompaniment of smiles and a shoulder slap, this pidgin passage was immediately acceptable to all the Japanese and Americans present as a slightly ribald joke meaning something like: "it's fine to look at the girl, but don't try anything else." (p. 53)

Another syntactic process in E J-Pidgin was the use of the same word for a variety of grammatical functions: *sayonara* could be used to mean "good bye," "to get rid of something" or "to assert the absence of something." Thus a jet mechanic said of a missing tool "This you speak sayonara?" meaning "Is this the one you said was missing?" An American housewife instructed her maid to throw away some leftovers by pointing to a garbage pail and saying "pailu sayonara it." (p. 53)

4. The lexicon of E J-Pidgin was often characterized by semantic extension:

a. *shimpai-nai* which derived from substandard Japanese for "no worry" was extended to a variety of meanings such as "don't bother," "let's enjoy ourselves," "you're welcome," "I've recovered from my malady."

b. English *okay* came to be used as a verb meaning "to fix" or "to adjust."

c. *no sukoshi* which in Japanese means a little more in either time or space, in E J-Pidgin came to mean "at a later time" or "after awhile." (p. 54)

Leachman and Hall (1955) discuss the features of American Indian Pidgin English (AIPE) from attestations of this form of speech found in literary and historical sources written between 1641 and 1946. Some of the characteristics of AIPE are:

1. Definite and indefinite articles are usually missing.

2. Possession is indicated by simple juxtaposition (white man mouth).
3. The verb structure is characterized by:
    a. general loss of inflectional features and the exclusive use of the simple form of the verb;
    b. *been* is used as the past of *be*; (This is similar to the use of *bin* as a past tense auxiliary in Neo-Melanesian.)
    c. repetition of the verb to indicate repeated action (court court; travel travel);
    d. copula deletion (Englishman much foole, that the best soldier, he cross);
    e. predicates are made negative by placing *no* before the center of the predicate (he no run away);
    f. the suffix / əm/ is widely used as a transitive suffix.
    g. the subject is recapitulated by a pronoun (rabbit, he hear that). This construction is similar to the predicate marker /i-/ in Neo-Melanesian.

Frederic Cassidy (1971) in an article called "The pidgin element in Jamaican Creole" speculates about the formation of pidgins. If secondary hybridization is considered genuine pidginization, then with some modification, the developmental process which he presents offers a suggestion for a sequence of development of the interlanguage of a second language learner:

1. Initially speech would be accompanied by a good deal of gesture (as was seen in English-Japanese Pidgin discussed above). The amount of gesture would gradually reduce, but would probably never be completely eliminated.

2. Due to the fact that parties involved in the communication would require identification, a personal pronoun system would develop to indicate *thou-you* and *I-we* relationships first and subsequently *he-they* relationships. In order to point out both things and people demonstrative pronouns would soon follow the personal pronouns. The near-far distinction would probably evolve first to indicate *this* and *that*.

3. Statements, questions, commands and requests would all require expression early in the development. Intonation and context would probably be used to distinguish them.

4. Another necessity would be to name things. The lexicon of one's job or profession would probably be the first learned and then it would extend to the more general environment and include words referring to time, numbers, weights and measures, colors,

kinship, body parts, tools and utensils, clothing, local wild life, and emotions. Verbs for thought and communication (know, say, forget); bodily motion (walk, stand, come, etc.); physical action (do, give, eat, look, etc.) and feelings (want, like, wonder, etc.) would be acquired.

5. Modification would have to develop and would include such ideas as: size; quality (good, strong, hot, etc.); condition and manner (ill, asleep, wet, hard, etc.); shape; position; direction and time (right-now, in-a-while, after, always, etc.).

6. Verbal expressions would first use only adverbs (yesterday/to-day/tomorrow/all-the-time, etc.) to express time relations. Later certain auxiliaries would probably be acquired to express these relations.

7. Even elementary communication would require the expression of possibilities, contingencies and causal relationships. Therefore the speaker would have to acquire and/or adapt syntax to express these relationships (Cassidy 1971, pp. 212-215).

If we accept the hypothesis that the early stages of free second language acquisition involve pidginization, the data presented by Smith, Goodman, Leachman and Hall, and Cassidy yield interesting hypotheses about what to expect in the interlanguage of second language learners. Continuing to speculate about the acquisition process, it appears that there may be a universal simplification process that operates in the acquisition of second language, perhaps under the control of what Selinker has called "a latent psychological structure" of the brain. This process will result in similarities in the early interlanguages of all free second language learners. What variation does appear in those interlanguages will be largely a product of the sociolinguistic conditions under which the language is learned. Using the notion of solidarity as developed by Joos (1971), we can predict that the extent of simplification and reduction which we observe in a learner's interlanguage will be the result of both the actual and potential social and psychological solidarity that exists between the language learner and the speakers of the target language. Developmental sequences in second language acquisition may vary according to differences in that solidarity.

1.3 *Complication and Expansion*

The simplification in morphology, reduction in vocabulary and deletion of certain grammatical transformations which are characteristic of pidgins tend to give way when the function of the pidgin is extended from communicative to integrative and expressive use. When a pidgin is creolized, i.e., when it becomes the first language of a group of speakers, it must serve all three language functions. It becomes a vehicle for marking one's social identity and expressing psychological needs and states. Concomitant with this extension in function is the complication and expansion of the language structure. (Smith 1971) It is the thesis of this chapter that when the language learner attempts to use his interlanguage for integrative and expressive purposes it will complicate and expand in ways similar to creolization. Redundancy will increase, obligatory tense markers will tend to develop, speed in speech will increase as a result of morphophonemic reductions and reductions in primary stress, and finally the lexicon will usually undergo extensive development.

Gillian Sankoff and Suzanne Laberge (1971) examine the first three of these phenomena in relation to the adverb *bai* in an incipient creole which is evolving as Neo-Melanesian acquires a generation of native speakers.

Bai is the reduced form of the adverb *baimbai* (coming from English *by* <u>and</u> *by*). It appears to be evolving into a future tense marker. It never receives primary stress and the children for whom Neo-Melanesian is a native language show a tendency to place less stress on it than do adults. Thus they speak the language with greater speed and fluency. *Bai* is becoming a redundant grammatical feature. It is used in sentences with adverbs of time such as *klostu* "soon," *bihain* "later" and *nau* "right now." Its redundant character is also evident from its frequent use several times within a single sentence. In addition, *bai* appears to be an obligatory future marker. Both its redundancy and its obligatory character are evident from the following example where every verb except *wokim* carries the future marker.

Pes pikinini ia *bai* yu go wok long, – *bai* yu stap ia na *bai* you stap long banis kau bilong mi na *bai* taim mi dai *bai* yu lukautim na yu save wokim susu na *bai* yu givim long, wonem ia, stua, na *bai* ol i baim.

You, first son, will go and work in, – you'll stay on my cattle farm and when I die you'll look after it, and you'll keep milking them and you'll send it to the store, and the people will buy it. (p. 12)

Traugott (1972, pp. 36-37)[2] cites Agar and Lefebvre's (1972) suggestion that in the verbal system of creoles there is a predictable hierarchic relationship:

If there is one tense marker, it is future (e.g., first generation creole Tok Pisin); if there are two, they are future and past (Hawaiian Creole, Martinican Creole); if there are three markers, they are present, future and past.

Traugott also suggests that all creoles have aspectual markers which tend to be obligatory and perphrastic. English-based creoles have progressive markers and French-based creoles tend to have perfective markers although neither is necessarily excluded from the other language. (p. 37) These suggestions offer concrete hypotheses about what we might expect to find in the expanding interlanguage of second language learners.

2.0 Conclusion

Let's now examine the processes of simplification, reduction, complication and expansion as they appear in ordinary second language learning situations. In the initial stage of learning, when the function of the language of a second language learner is restricted to communication, we can expect the learner's interlanguage to reflect some of the simplifications and reductions that are found in pidgins. Longitudinal studies of second language acquisition are necessary to test this hypothesis, but nevertheless less formal observation seems to indicate that rejection of redundancy by neophyte language learners is extremely common. H. V. George (1972) reports:

> The difficulty of teachers of English to Asian children is that many of the children accept the features of English which seem to them to be nonredundant, and with these features make a *language of communication* which is more efficient than the standard English which they, the teachers, are attempting to teach. In other words, what for the teacher is "wrong" is for the learner psychologically correct. (p. 14) (Emphasis mine.)

This rejection of redundancy leads to a pidgin-like simplification in morphology that all language teachers have observed:

1. *Verb inflections*

   He play baseball everyday.
   He play baseball yesterday.
   He play baseball tomorrow.
   He play baseball now.
       or
   He playing baseball now.
       or
   He's play baseball now.

2. *Plural inflection*

   We have many pretty dress.
   He bought five book.
   I want these pencil.

3. *Possessive inflection*

He has John book.
We drive he father car.

Language learners also tend to delete certain grammatical transformations which appear redundant and thus they produce question forms similar to pidgins:

He open the door?
Where he put the book?
What she say?

The very common resistance to learning the passive voice may also stem from a rejection of redundancy and a desire to simplify. For purposes of communication, the passive simply represents another more complicated way of saying the same thing. The same process seems to underlie the acquisition of vocabulary. If two words have the same denotative meaning are presented, they will appear redundant and the language learner, at the early stages, will tend to use only of them.

It is only when a language learner develops an integrative motivation such that he wants to use his language to mark his social identity within the target culture or to express subtle psychological states or needs to native speakers of the target language, that the need for redundancy, alternate forms and stylistic variation becomes important. It is at this point, as Sankoff has pointed out in the development of Neo-Melanesian creole, that the speed and fluency of the second language learner increases, obligatory tense markers appear along with adverbs of time, and vocabulary expands to include synonyms with different connotata. Since classroom language learning forces the learner to focus on redundant features from the very beginning we have little data demonstrating the "creolization" of the second language learner's speech.

The longitudinal studies suggested by Corder should allow us to test the hypothesis that the learner language evolves from pidginization, to creolization, to eventual conformity with the target language norm. Nevertheless, it is a common observation that some second language learners never acquire a complicated and expanded interlanguage which eventually conforms to the target language. These learners continue to use simplified and reduced interlanguage in spite of long exposure to the target culture. The persistence of pidginized forms probably indicates that the function of the speakers' second language is still limited to communication. Expansion and complication will not take place until the function is extended to integrative and expressive use. This view is compatible with the findings of Wallace Lambert *et alia* (1970) which indicate that success in second language learning is the result of an integrative motivation (the desire to become like the speakers of the target language) rather than instrumental motivation (language learning for utilitarian reasons such as mere survival or getting ahead in one's occupation).

In order to confirm the "interlanguage hypothesis" as developed by Corder, Selinker and Nemser or to establish that the development of the learner language is analogous to pidginization and creolization, longitudinal studies of second language acquisition will have to be made. Both the interlanguage hypothesis and the pidginization-creolization model offer very clear suggestions of what to look for in such studies.

This article is published for the first time in this volume. A version of the article called, "The Implications of Interlanguage, Pidginization and Creolization for the Study of Adult Second Language Acquisition", also appeared in *TESOL Quarterly*, Vol. 8, No. 2, June 1974, pp. 145-152.

FOOTNOTES

[1]Professor Traugott has some reservations on this point. She believes, however, that the shallowness of derivation is predictable from the fact that function is restricted (personal communication).

[2]Professor Traugott, however, feels that this hypothesis is extremely odd since one would hardly expect futures (being marked in most languages) to be the only markers. Also the hypothesis is not really generalizable from Tok Pisin (the only example) to all creoles (personal communication).

BIBLIOGRAPHY

Agar, Elaine and Claire Lefebvre. Verb forms in pidgins and creoles. University of California, Berkeley, June 1972.

Bever, Thomas G. and D. Terence Langendoen. A dynamic model of the evolution of language. *Linguistic Inquiry*, Vol. 2, No. 4, Fall 1971, pp. 433-464.

Cassidy, Frederic G. Tracing the pidgin element in Jamaican Creole. In Hymes (ed.), *Pidginization and Creolization of Languages*. Cambridge University Press, 1971, pp. 203-221.

Corder, S. P. Describing the language learner's language. *Interdisciplinary Approaches to Language.* CILT Reports and Papers 6, September 1971b, pp. 57-64.

Corder, S. P. Idiosyncratic dialects and error analysis. *International Review of Applied Linguistics*, Vol. 9, No. 2, 1971a, pp. 147-159.

Corder, S. P. The significance of learner's errors. *International Review of Applied Linguistics*, Vol. 4, 1967, pp. 161-169.

Decamp, David. Introduction: The Study of Pidgin and Creole Languages. In Hymes (ed.), *Pidginization and Creolization of Languages.* Cambridge University Press, 1971, pp. 14-39.

Ferguson, Charles A. Absence of copula and the notion of simplicity: a study of normal speech, baby talk, foreigner talk, and pidgins. In Hymes (ed.), *Pidginization and Creolization of Languages.* Cambridge University Press, 1971, pp. 141-149.

George, H. V. *Common Errors in Learning English.* Rowley, Massachusetts: Newbury House Publishers, 1972.

Goodman, John S. The development of a dialect of English-Japanese pidgin. *Anthropological Linguistics*, Vol. 9, No. 6, 1967, pp. 43-55.

Hall, R. A. Jr. *Pidgin and Creole Languages.* Ithaca, Cornell University Press, 1966.

Hymes, Dell (ed.). *Pidginization and Creolization of Languages.* Cambridge University Press, 1971.

Joos, Martin. Hypotheses as to the origin and modification of pidgins. In Hymes, (ed.), *Pidginization and Creolization of Languages.* Cambridge University Press, 1971, p. 187.

Kay, Paul and Gillian Sankoff. A language-universals approach to pidgins and creoles. 23rd Georgetown Roundtable on languages and linguistics, 1972.

Lambert, W. E., R. C. Gardner, R. Olton and K. Tunstull. A study of the roles of attitudes and motivation in second language learning. In Fishman (ed.), *Readings in the Sociology of Language.* The Hague: Mouton Press, 1970, pp. 473-491.

Leachman, Douglas and Hall, Robert A. Jr. American Indian Pidgin English: attestations and grammatical peculiarities. *American Speech*, Vol. 30, No. 3, 1955, pp. 163-171.

Nemser, W. Approximative systems of foreign language learners. *International Review of Applied Linguistics*, Vol. 9, No. 2, pp. 115-123.

Sankoff, Gillian and Suzanne Laberge. On the acquisition of native speakers by a language. Mimeo, 1971.

Selinker, Larry. Interlanguage. *International Review of Applied Linguistics*, Vol. 10, No., 3, 1972, pp. 209-231.

Smith, David M. Some implications for the social status of pidgin languages. Mimeo, 1971 (since published in *Sociolinguistics in Cross-Cultural Analysis*, David M. Smith and Roger W. Shuy, editors, Georgetown University Press, Washington, D.C., 1972).

Traugott, Elizabeth Closs. Historical linguistics and its relation to studies of language acquisition and of pidgins and creoles. Mimeo, 1972.

Whinnom, Keith. Linguistic hybridization and the 'special case' of pidgins and creoles. In Hymes (ed.), *Pidginization and Creolization of Languages*. Cambridge University Press, 1971, pp. 91-115.

I.

THE DEVELOPMENT OF WH-QUESTIONS IN FIRST AND SECOND LANGUAGE LEARNERS[1]

ROAR RAVEM

1.0 *Introduction*

Roger Brown (1968)[2] reports the result of an analysis of Wh-questions in the speech of the three children whose language development has been studied by him and his associates at Harvard University.[3] The analysis was made to determine whether or not there was evidence in the spontaneous speech of preschool children that the transformational rules of current generative-transformational grammar also figure in the child's competence, in other words, if the intermediate hypothetical strings in a transformational analysis correspond to stages in the child's development of Wh-questions. Such hypothetical intermediates are not, usually, actualized in adult forms and hence not available to the child for imitation. If they occurred in the speech of children at a certain stage of development, it would suggest that transformational grammar has managed to capture psychologically real operations, and it would throw further doubt on an empiricist explanation of language acquisition, since these intermediate structures are not exemplified in the language data the child is exposed to.

2.0 *The Grammar of Wh-Questions*

Table 1 presents examples of types of sentences that I shall be concerned with in this report, here given in their adult form.

TABLE 1

When will John come?
What was Mary saying?
Where has he gone?
How do you like it?
Why did John leave?
Who did Mary see?
Who saw John?

In the current transformation analysis the sentences in Table 1 are derived transformationally from a final derived phrase marker (a terminal string of symbols derived by phrase structure rules). The leftmost symbol will be an abstract interrogative morpheme (Q), followed by the subject noun phrase (NP) and the verb phrase (VP). Each of these major constituents will dominate a hierarchy of minor constituents. Thus the VP will contain an AUX, which contains tense (T) and a verbal auxiliary constituent. It will further include to the right of AUX a main verb (V) and an NP when the sentence requires a direct object. If the sentence requires an adverbial (ADV), this will be generated to the right of the VP. The constituent to be questioned, either the subject NP or the object NP or the Adv, will have associated with it an abstract dummy element (WH).[4] Before lexical insertion, a simplified underlying string for a sentence like

When will John read the book?

would look like this:

Q   NP   AUX   V   NP   WH-ADV (time)

For convenience we will render it as:

Q   John will read the book WHEN?

In this example the constituent ADV has been questioned. If an NP is questioned, we get either *Q   John will read WHAT* or *Q   WHO will read the book.*

To derive the normal question, two transformations are required (disregarding the transformation that deletes Q), namely, (1) a "preposing transformation", which moves the constituent with the WH-feature to a front position (this transformation applies vacuously when it is the subject NP that contains the WH-feature), and (2) a "transposing transformation", which moves (the first element of) the auxiliary in front of the subject NP. *Q   John will read WHAT*   will by (1) be changed into

WHAT John will read?

and further by (2)

WHAT will John read?

If morpho-phonemic rules were applied to the underlying non-transformed strings, sentences like the following would result:

John will read what?
John will read the book when?
Who will read the book?

If we assume that the stages in language acquisition mirror the transformational derivation in transformational grammar, we would expect to find sentences in the child's grammar that are basically of this form. I shall therefore refer to it as the first Hypothetical Intermediate (H.I.1).

It should be noted, however, that the H.I.1 is not identical with Brown's "Occasional Question" (1968, p. 279). In Brown's treatment the *Wh*-word is spoken with heavy stress and rising intonation. He gives the following example. "If someone said: 'John will read the telephone book' one might respond 'John will read *what?*' ". This would not in my analysis constitute an example of H.I.1. As a question it is semantically different from a normal question in that the constituent that is questioned is already known and the question expresses a disbelief or astonishment.[5] The sentence we would expect to find, if our assumption were correct, would be one with normal interrogative stress and intonation.

The next stage of development would be one in which morpho-phonemic rules were applied to an underlying string after preposing, but in the absence of transposing. This would result in sentences like:

What John will read?
When John will read the book?

I shall refer to this type as the second Hypothetical Intermediate (H.I.2). It corresponds to the Hypothetical Intermediate found to be a general feature of the grammar of the three children studied by Brown and his associates.

Diagram 1 is meant to illustrate some of the features relevant to our discussion of the underlying structures of *Wh*-questions as they might be represented in a child's grammar. The Q symbolizes the fact that a sentence is to be interpreted as a question; the constituent to be questioned has received the feature +WH. If the constituent at the NP node has the additional feature +human, the lexical item to be chosen will be *Who*; if it is -human, the lexical item will be *What*. Similarly, the features associated with the +WH of the ADV node will ultimately generate the lexical items *Where, When, How,* and *Why* respectively.

DIAGRAM 1

The diagram on the following page has been designed for expository convenience; details have therefore been omitted and notational conventions violated. (a)-(f) exemplify structures underlying the hypothetically intermediate strings (H.I.1) in Table 2.

DIAGRAM 1

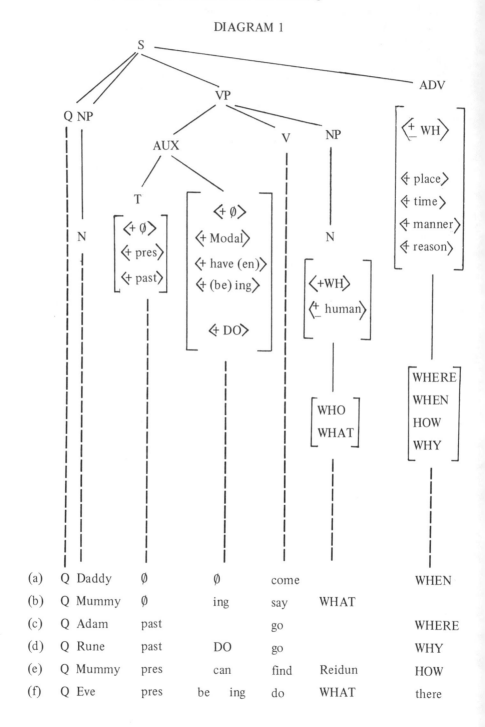

The rules of the grammar will up to this point generate sentences of the form illustrated by Table 2.

TABLE 2

(a)   Daddy come when?
(b)   Mummy saying what?
(c)   Adam goed where?
(d)   Rune did go why?
(e)   Mummy can find Reidun how?
(f)   Eve are doing what there?

Brown's prediction that sentences of this type would be the first to emerge after the initial pretransformational stage was not borne out by the result of his analysis of the material. "In fact, that was not the next step—at least not the next step we could see, the next step in performance. Occasional questions never became frequent for the children, and the first ones appeared somewhat later than [Level] III. This may be entirely a matter of grammatical performance, of what the children found "occasion" to say rather than of competence or what they were able to say. As we shall see, the occasions on which these forms are used are special and may simply not have arisen for the child" (1968, p. 284). This explanation seems reasonable, *provided* the occasional form is a true occasional form with the special suprasegmental features and semantic connotations that Brown implies. Our main hypothesis, however, would predict sentences of the H.I.1 type as the normal interrogative form at one stage of development, but *without* special stress and intonation features superimposed on them, e.g., such sentences as: *You going where, Mummy?, Eve doing what, Adam?, Adam goed where, Daddy?,* Presumably no examples of this kind have been found by Brown, which means that neither Brown's hypothesis about occasional questions nor mine about H.I.1 has been confirmed by Brown's study.[6]

The story is different for our H.I.2, which is the string resulting from a preposing transformation. An actualization of this string would change the sentences in Table 2 to those in Table 3.

TABLE 3

(a)   When Daddy come?
(b)   What Mummy saying?
(c)   Where Adam goed?
(d)   Why Rune did go?
(e)   How Mummy can find Reidun?
(f)   What Eve are doing there?

The sentences in Table 3 are not actual sentences from a corpus, but they are—with the possible exception of (d)—plausible children's sentences. All the three children in the study reported by Brown used sentences of the preposing type, so here at least the hypothesis is not disconfirmed.

3.0 Own Study[7]

The findings to be described in this survey are based on a preliminary analysis of the emergence of Wh-questions in the speech of two Norwegian children learning English as a second language in a naturalistic setting. i.e., in an English-speaking environment comparable to that of first language learners, with the exception that Norwegian is usually spoken at home.

The two studies have been longitudinal-observational and the corpora consist of tape-recorded interviews and various informal experiments, mainly translation and imitation tests.

My informants have been my son, Rune, and my daughter, Reidun. Rune was 6 1/2 when the study began and he had a rudimentary knowledge of English from a previous stay in Great Britain. The material for this study was collected over a period of five months, with fairly intensive recordings at 3-4 week intervals. For a report based on part of the corpus see Ravem (1968).

My present study is a follow-up of the previous study, but has mainly concentrated on my daughter's acquisition of English. She was three years and nine months old when the study began in September 1968. At that time she had no knowledge of English. Her Norwegian language development has on a subjective impression been normal and average. Her articulation has been exceptionally clear in both languages, which has facilitated transcriptions and made them more reliable.[8] The recordings were made at weekly intervals up to July 1969, each interview averaging one hour.

The interlocutors have been either our eldest, bilingual daughter, my wife and myself, native English-speaking adults, or playmates. The interviews have been arranged without being deliberately structured, as I wanted the speech during the sessions to be as spontaneous as possible. The most rewarding situations with regard to amount of data have been with peers or members of the family. As we were conscious about what we were looking for, we could steer the conversations in different directions and thereby elicit responses of the kind we were interested in. The translation tests have proved a useful instrument for eliciting the types of sentences I wanted, and their validity has been supported by obtained utterances in free conversation.

The collection of material was resumed after a break of two months, when the family was in Norway. Intensive recordings were made immediately before and after the break, as I was interested in the degree of forgetting that might have occurred during the two months. This, however, is only an incidental aspect of the study. Reidun seemed essentially to have caught up with her agemates by July 1969, but the collection of material has continued since in a less systematic fashion. I have only recently started analyzing the corpus and the present report is based on only a portion of it.

4.0 *Results and Discussion*

There is no *prima facie* evidence why a child acquiring a second language should go through a similar development as first language learners. Nor incidentally, is it obvious that essentially the same path is followed (the same strategy chosen) by all learners of their mother tongue. Although a comprehensive study, the investigation by Brown and associates is to my knowledge the only complete longitudinal study of interrogative and negative sentences to date, and it comprises only three children. It is therefore quite conceivable that the picture will be more varied as more studies have been undertaken.

Nevertheless, as the actual data in Tables 4 and 5 show there are striking similarities between my own material and data from the study by Brown and associates (Table 6), and it is not likely that this is altogether accidental. (If one set out to search for differences, these would probably be equally striking, but less surprising). I have not yet found any examples corresponding to our H.I.1; nor have I found any of Brown's occasional questions, with their associated stress and intonation contour, in spite of the fact that they are quite frequent in the speech of the interlocutors (my wife and myself).

TABLE 4. Wh-questions from Rune#Times 1-4

Time 1   What is that?
What are mean? (what does mean mean)
Where is that /britʃ/? ("brikke")
What you eating?
What he's doing?
What she is doing?
What—you going to build tomorrow?
Where dem drink?
Why you say that before? (for)

Time 2   What Jane give him?
(c. 2 wks.   Rannveig, what dyou doing to-yesterday on school?
later)   What dyou like?
        (Adult: Say that again clearly)
        'What 'you' like?
        What you think Pappy—name is?
        What is—Mummy doing not?

(T)   What you doing to-yesterday?
(T)   What dyou do to-yesterday?
(T)   What you going to do tomorrow?
(T)   What-uh-time-uh-clock Rannveig come back?
        (when; fut. re.)
(T)   What you talking to to-yesterday? (who)

Time 3   What. . .you knitting?
(3-4 wks.   What he's doing?
later)   What is he doing?
        What dyou do the last week before you be—
            did—"bli"—ill?

(T)   What dyou reading to-yesterday?
        What you did in Rothbury?
        What dyou did to-yesterday in the hayshed?
        How did you do—have do—you—do—what you do
            on school last week?
        When dyou went there? (In response to: Ask her
            when she went there)
        Why the baby crying?
        Why he come for a cup of coffee?
        Why dyou must have table—and chairs?
        Why drink we tea and coffee?
(T)   Why we not live in Scotland?
(T)   Why not Mummy make dinner?

Time 4   What you did after Ranny go to bed? (In response
(c. 3 wks.   to: Ask Dad what he did?)
later)   What did you more—that night?
        What did you talk to them? (say/talk about)
(T)   What do you doing to-yesterday?
(T)   What did you do to-yesterday?
        When you go to bed? (past reference)
(T)   What do you going to do tomorrow?
(T)   Who you talking to to-yesterday?
(T)   Why not that go up? (that window)
        Why not Mummy make meat today? (from Nor.
            "mat" = food)

        (T) stands for Translation Test.

TABLE 5. Wh-questions from Reidun

Months: weeks
of exposure
to English

3:1   What this? (What color is this)

4:0   Where find it? (in response to: Ask her. . .where
            you can find it)
        Where "jeg kan jeg" find it—apples? (jeg = I;
            kan = can)

4:4   Whats that?
        "Hvor er"—my Mummy? (where is)

5:3   Whats her doing?
        Whats "er" her doing? (er = is/are)
        Where "er" hers Mummy?
        Why that the bed "er" broken? (prob.: why (is
            it) that)

6:0   What that is?
        Why it—Humpty Dumpty sat on a horse?

6:2   What call that man?
        What—name that man?
        Why that man have that on?
        Whats that—is?
        Why—uh—him have got like that? (a jacket like
            that)
        Why her don't stand there?
        "Hvem er" that? (who)
        Whos that?
        Whos that is?
        Whosis that is?
        What her going to make? (or: goingto?)
        Whats her baking?

6:3   Which one you want?
        What you want?
        What do you want? (or: doyou)

8:0   Who is that?
        Why you can't buy like that shoes?
        Where is it, then?
        Whats are they?
        Why him have got a motor?
        Why you can't—why you couldn't take it here?
            (i.e., bring)
        What I got on?
        Why I got that white dress on?

Mummy, where—where was you—are?
Where my penny?

9:3   What they got on they eyes?
What are he doing now, then—that man?
Why isn't that lady in there?
Why can't you touch with your—with your hand?
Which color have we got, then?
Whats those two man doing?
What they doing?
Why hasn't she—got same as us?

TABLE 6. Wh-questions from the study by R. Brown and associates*

Stage 2   Where my mitten?
Where me sleep?
What the dollie have?
What book name?
Why you smiling?
Why not me sleeping?
Why not. . .me can't dance?

Stage 3   Where's his other eye?
Where I should put it when I make it up?
Where my spoon goed?
What I did yesterday?
What he can ride in?
What did you doed?
Why the Christmas tree going?
Why Paul caught it?
Why he don't know how to pretend?
Why kitty can't stand up?
Which way they should go?
How he can be a doctor?
How that opened?
How they can't talk?

*The examples are taken from E. S. Klima and U. Bellugi (1966). Klima and Bellugi's Stages do not correspond to Brown's Levels. Stage 2 appears to correspond roughly to Level III.

Brown's discussion of the role of the occasional form might play in helping the child to see the relationship between different, but equivalent, question forms; the relation of the *Wh*-word to various pro-forms, such as *it* and *there*; and to learn the membership of a constituent, such as NP, is an interesting and plausible attempt to show that there is more in the language data the child is exposed to than meets the ear and that one might profitably look again at what might be exemplified in the input before one jumps to "innateness" conclusions. However, the discussion would appear to be much less relevant to L2 acquisition, where the abstract categories and relationships are already known to the child through his first language. The learning task of my children may have been more of the order of learning how these relations, or whatever, are realized in the second language.

It appears, then, that transformational grammar has captured a stage in the child's development of Wh-questions; but this is not the same as saying that it has captured a psychologically real operation. The latter is what Brown, in effect, assumes. "We believe that these questions, in general, were derived by a single preposing transformation out of underlying strings with dummy elements..." (1968, p. 286). The preposing transformation cannot be given a psychological status without at the same time assuming some kind of psychological reality for the underlying string (H.I.1). If this were not the case, there would be no preposing operation to carry out. It is for the hypothesis unfortunate that no sentences have been obtained that could be said to be either an actualization of the occasional question or of our II.I.1.

While entertaining the hypothesis of a preposing operation, Brown goes on to discuss the evidence for and against it. The Wh-questions in his corpus fall into two classes, one which he calls "Preposing Weak" and another which he calls "Preposing Strong". A general characteristic of children's early speech is the omission of inflections and of minor word classes (functors), which results in what has been referred to as "telegraphic" speech (Brown and Fraser 1963). The class for which the evidence for a preposing transformation is weak consists of children's sentences that could have been learned as a reduction of adult speech to "telegraphese", as shown by the following examples, where the omitted words are in parentheses:

What (do) you want?
How (will) you open it?
What (is) his name?

The second class if Wh-questions are those for which the evidence for a preposing operation is strong, since they cannot be arrived at by telegraphic reduction. This is the case where the verb is inflected or where the questions include auxiliaries or the verb *be*, for example:

What he wants?
How he opened it?
What you will want?
Why you can't open it?
What his name is?

Before we consider the validity of the evidence for a preposing operation, it might be profitable to ask why one would want to suggest a hypothesis of this kind in the first place. If I understand Brown correctly, the argument seems to run something like this: The children had prior to Level III produced large numbers of Wh-questions, with all the Wh-words in initial position, but there was reason to believe that the questions were constructions or routines of some non-transformational type.[9] At Level III, however, there is ample evidence that the Wh-word replaces missing elements in the sentence, both locative adverbials and subject and object noun phrases. The child is capable of responding appropriately to questions calling for different constituents and is also able to produce such questions. "It seems then that the constituents were organized as such and that the children were able to take a Wh word supplied by a parent as the signal to supply an appropriate constituent member." (1968, p. 284).

The child's "knowledge" can thus be accounted for by transformational grammar; but why would one expect to find that this knowledge—for which there is independent evidence—should be demonstrated in the child's language as an actualization of either the occasional question or H.I.1? Brown expected to find it since the occasional question "only requires that the dummy element (which becomes a Wh word) be selected from the constituent and supplied in place" (ibid.). I did not expect to find it, since the child has already for a long time used Wh-words in initial position and since the Wh-word normally appears in the same position in the adult model. What I am uneasy about in Brown's analysis, is that it appears to tie position learning of a fairly simple kind too closely to a much more abstract form of learning complex interrelationships. We can independently establish that the child possesses knowledge of the kind made explicit by transformation grammar and choose to describe it in those terms, and, for example, say that the child "knows" that *what* in *What you want?* is the direct object of *want* and that it is related to an indefinite Proform in the declarative sentence *You want 'something'*. It seems to me that it is quite legitimate to assume this knowledge and at the same time propose hypotheses to account for the order of constituents in Wh-questions of the preposing type in the child's speech.

One such hypothesis suggests itself, namely that the Wh-word remains in initial position and is followed by a "nucleus" which retains the word order of a declarative sentence according to the child's grammar at any time.[10] This hypothesis does not purport to account for more than word order; nor is there more involved, it seems to me, in Brown's class of weak evidence. The evidence for preposing is weak exactly because it allows for an explanation in terms of selective imitation of an adult model and leaves unanswered such questions as how the child is able to question different constituents or can see the relationship between discontinuous constituents, such as the verb and the direct object in *What you want?*

The Preposing Weak class constitutes weak evidence for preposing only if the "strong" evidence that Brown alleges does exist. If one is willing to concede an alternative explanation which is not in terms of an "underlying grammatical network" for the Preposing Weak class, one should do this also for the class of strong evidence. On the alternative hypothesis (Wh Nucleus) the strong evidence will turn out to be no stronger than the weak evidence; the hypothesis does not, in fact, distinguish between them. Sentences like *What he wants?* or *Why you can't open it?* cannot be derived from adult models alone, but the "nucleus" of the sentence (or what remains of it) preserves the word order of the declarative sentence. When the child acquires inflections and auxiliaries in declarative sentences these will also—although usually somewhat later, which may complicate the analysis—be incorporated in Wh-questions as well. This alternative explanation does not affect the hypothesis that the child reduces adult speech in a systematic way and induces general rules on the basis of this reduction; but by adopting reduction as the only criterion, one is forced into setting up a separate class of Preposing Strong evidence, which is not required by the alternative hypothesis.

I like to believe that Tables 4 and 5 show, fairly conclusively, that the intermediate sentence type without transposing (inversion) is a feature also of my informants' acquisition of English as a second language. That they already knew the transposing transformation from Norwegian does not seem to have had much effect. Admittedly, the majority of the sentences obtained before inversion became general were of the Preposing Weak type, and hence could have resulted from reduction alone. Even if that were the case, one would have to account for the many clear cases of lack of inversion, such as:

> What that is?
> What she is doing?
> What you did in Rothbury?
> Why that man have that on?

A difficulty in deciding whether or not the lack of transposing represents a necessary developmental stage is the fact, which Brown also notes (ibid., p. 285), that by the time the child produces sentences of the Preposing Strong type, he might already have gone a long way to acquiring the adult form with inversion. There are several examples in Table 5 that show how Reidun oscillates between different alternatives, e.g.:

> (6:2) "Hvem er" that? (Who is that)
> Whos that?
> Whos that is?
> Whosis that is?

It does not seem unreasonable to expect that my children would have made use of inversion from the beginning by applying the rules for Norwegian. There are isolated examples from both Rune and Reidun where this is in fact the case, e.g.:

> Why drink we tea and coffee? (Rune)
> Where livd (i.e., live) Catherine and Richard? (Reidun)

but they remain isolated cases. Lack of inversion was a feature of Reidun's Norwegian at an intermediate stage in her development as well, so we seem to have to do with a rather general phenomenon.[11] Since the use of the auxiliary *do* is specific to English, I will return to the acquisition of it later; I only want to point out here that there is strong evidence that *dyou* in Rune's speech, probably throughout Time 3, was a variant of *you*. The examples with *dyou* in Table 4 are therefore only apparent counter-examples of transposing.

5.0 *The Development of the AUX node*

Diagram 1 shows that the AUX is the most "crowded" node on our tree. It contains some morphemes that are lexical and others that are realized as inflections, for example, present or past tense, past participle (en), and present participle (ing). There are a number of combinatorial possibilities, some as complicated as, for example:

> *Past Modal have en be ing*

Even without considering the cognitive problems involved in

acquiring tense and aspect, the linguistic mechanisms themselves are complicated enough, and it is therefore to be expected that the full range of auxiliary morphemes and their distribution will be late in developing. There is probably room for some individual variation in the order in which children develop the AUX node, but the general picture is from no auxiliary at all through stages of approximations to adult grammar. I have not yet done any detailed analysis of the development of the auxiliary in my children, but it seems to resemble in many important respects the development in first language learners.

The main function of *do* is to be a carrier of tense.[12] The task of the learner of English is to discover this particular function of *do*. Since the use of *do* is specific to English, the second language learner is faced with very much the same learning problem. *Do* has been included in Diagram 1 as a verbal element of AUX, because it shares some of the distributional characteristics of the Modals. We could therefore on this basis predict that Wh-questions at the H.I.2 stage would have the form of sentence (d), *Why Rune did go?*, in Table 3, namely:

WH   NP   Tense-Do V

When *do* was introduced in affirmative Wh-questions as a tense carrier, Rune used inversion, for example:

What did you do before you get to bed?

With Reidun the situation is not as clear-cut. There is still much material that has not been analyzed, and although a couple of her affirmative Wh-questions have inversion of *do* and the subject NP (Table 5, 9:3), the translation tests show isolated examples of the translation tests show isolated examples of non-inversion, e.g.:

(8:4) *Where we did livd for we come here?*
         (for = before)

I would have tended to interpret the few examples of non-inversion of *do* and subject NP in Wh-questions found so far as possible performance mistakes had it not been for Reidun's widespread use of *do* in declarative sentences, which might suggest a prior (or optional) rule of non-transposing also in Wh-questions with the auxiliary *do*. Examples are:

(9:1) I did have jelly.
(9:2) My Mummy did make lunch for them.
      You did take me, didn't you?
      . . .and she did say 'yes', she did.
      We did saw that in the shop.

Nuclear stress is in none of the entries on *did*, so there is no question of an emphatic form. Menyuk (1969, p. 73) gives an example from first language learners of both an affirmative sentence with *do* and a Wh-question without inversion:

> I did read that motor boat book.
> Where the wheel do go?

6.0 *Why and Why not Questions*

Although formally identical to other Wh-questions of the preposing type, Brown (1968, pp. 286-7) found reason to suspect that *Why*- and *Why not*-questions were not derived "by a single preposing transformation out of underlying strings with dummy elements" when they were first introduced by Adam, one of his three informants. Adam's responses did not give evidence that he related his questions to a missing constituent, but rather to his mother's antecedent declarative, e.g.:

MOTHER	ADAM
I see a seal.	Why Adam see seal?
I don't see anything.	Why not you see anything?
You can't dance.	Why not me can't dance?

The underlying constituent that is questioned in *Why (not)*-questions is the indefinite proform "for some reason". The answers to such questions are clauses involving causal or teleological explanations introduced by "because" or "in order that". It is therefore not implausible that *Why (not)*- questions are introduced at a later stage than other question types and that there is no clear relationship between the interrogative word and the questioned constituent in these questions when they first appear in the child's speech. In Adam's case it seems likely that he had some vague notion about causality, but that he is dependent upon an antecedent declarative sentence, which he largely echoes (using his own grammar) and to which he preposes *Why* or *Why not*. As for the two other children in the study, they did not start producing *Why (not)*-questions till they had reached the stage when they could give appropriate answers to them.

This appears, from a survey of parts of my corpus, to have been the case also with Reidun. Early *Why*- questions did not receive an appropriate response.

> RUNE: Why do you put the telephone on the front seat?
> (3:2) REIDUN: Yes.

Reidun's acquisition of *Why*-questions and their appropriate responses cannot in the same way as for first language learners be related to her cognitive development, that is, to "learning what explanation is". She knew this, relative to her age, and had used the Norwegian equivalents for some time.

As Table 7 shows, all Reidun's early sentences lack inversion. The first attested occurrences of Why-questions were in the fifth month of exposure to English. One half-hour recording at 6:3 had no less than 27 *Why-* questions and 8 *Why not*-questions. In the same recording there were three "because"-responses and two embedded "because"-clauses. The *Why (not)-* questions corresponded both to Brown's Preposing Weak and Preposing Strong types. Since Reidun had by now acquired auxiliaries and inflections required by the Preposing Strong class, a large percentage of her sentences were of this type.

TABLE 7. *Why (not)-* questions from Reidun

Months: weeks
of exposure
to English

	6:2	Why that man have got it?
		Why uh that horses have that—that on—foot?
		Why—that man are over there?
		Why her don't stand there?
	7:2	Why that man take—hang clothes on the—on the boat?
		Why that go up?
	7:3	Why you can't eat it?
	8:0	Why I sitting there?
		Why Daddy hold me?
		Why we can't go to London now—today?
	8:2	Why has him lotsome pockets?
		Why them have got some—lotsome pockets?
		Why "de" got those on?
		Why can't I have it?
		Why you've got those paper?
(T)	8:4	Why. . .Rune. . .isn't here?
		Why Toto don't cry?
		Why Andy Pandy don't sleep yet—now?
		Why Daddy don't "lag" (i.e., make)—eat lunch tomorrow? (i.e., yesterday)

(T)   9:2   Why isn't Rune here?
               Why doesn't Toto. . .cry?
               Why isn't Andy Pandy sleeping?
               . . .Why didn't Daddy—make lunch—yesterday?

       9:2   Why have you got it on?
               Why must I sit on the floor?
               Why is it too hot?

The first clear case of inversion in the material so far analyzed occurred at 8:2, viz.,

               Why has him lotsome pockets?

which was followed soon after by the non-inverted

               Why them have got some—lotsome pockets?

At 8:4 most of the *Why* (*not*)- questions in the translation test were of the Preposing Strong type, and none of them had undergone transposing:

               Why Toto is in him room?
               Why we don't go to Norway?
               Why Daddy haven't got hat on?
               Why I must bath all - all day? (i.e., every day)

The change took place at about 9:0 months of exposure, possible affecting the copular sentences first. By 9:2 all the entries in the translation test had inversion (but not all Wh-questions):

               Why is Toto up his room?
               Why don't we go in Norway?
               Why haven't Daddy got hat on - his head?
               Why must I - bath all day?

Because of the many occurrences of transposing noticed during the interview session a few days later (9:2), some elicited imitation items were added at the end of the session, such as:

FATHER: Why you didn't go to Colchester?
REIDUN: Why didn't you go to Colchester?

FATHER: Why she has got trousers on?
REIDUN: Why have you got trousers on?

FATHER: Why Mummy doesn't sit on the table?
REIDUN: Why doesn't Mummy sit on the table?

It appears, then, that the transposing operation took place over a short period of time and seems to have affected both affirmative and negative *Why*-questions with different auxiliaries simultaneously.

    All Adam's early negative *Why*-questions were declarative sentences preposed by *Why not.* The introduction of an initial *Why not* has tentatively been suggested by Bellugi as a developmental stage in the formation of negative questions, which might in turn have been responsible for the temporary use of double negation by the children, such as, *Why not me can't dance?*[13] As the examples cited from Reidun show, the basis for her negative *Why-* questions is *Why* followed by a negative nucleus, and I have found no double negatives at this stage.

Rune, however, produced negative questions of both types, either

> *Why Nucleus (neg)*

or

> *Why not Nucleus*

for example:

> Why you not come home?
> Why not that window go up?

Either type was produced throughout Times 3-5 in a crude translation test, apparently in a random fashion. Although there is little data on *Why not*-questions from Rune's first stay in Great Britain, there is supporting evidence in the—as yet unanalyzed—data from the beginning of his second stay to suggest that they were alternative patterns. Although the auxiliary *do* had appeared in Rune's *What*-questions at Time 4, there were no occurrences of *do* in the elicited *Why not-* questions. This might be accidental, or due to the fact that negative questions are more complicated, involving a negative transformation in addition.

Rune's further development could have been based on either of the structures *Why Nucleus (neg)* or *Why not Nucleus*, exemplified by *Why you not like ice-cream?* and *Why not you like ice-cream?* If the next stage in Rune's development involved the introduction of *do* without transposing—which would be conceivable, taking the timing of the two operations in Rune's speech into account—we could predict sentences of either or both of the following kind:

(i)   Why you don't like ice-cream?
(ii)   Why not you don't like ice-cream?

Although there are a few unprocessed tape-recordings from the period between Time 5 (the end of March 1966), when my study was discontinued, and July 1966, when our first stay in Great Britain was terminated, I have no analysis as yet of Rune's speech from that three-month period. However, when preparing my report (1968) in January 1967, I devised some translation test items for Rune in order to find out what had happened to his *Why*-questions after he had been away from English for half a year. I expected that I would find non-inverted sentences, mainly of type (i) above. As shown by the following examples, this expectation was not borne out:

> Why do we not live in Oslo?
> Why doesn't we go to Oslo?
> Why doesn't Reidun cry?
> Why did you not draw that letter to grandma? (i.e., write)

There were a few occurrences of more primitive structures, such as, *Why not Ranny come home?*, as well as double negatives, the status of which is difficult to ascertain, for example, *Why didn't Mummy don't make dinner to-yesterday?*. (They could reflect a combination of transposing with a negative nucleus; or they could simply be performance mistakes. No attempt was made at the time to find out.)

These examples show that Rune had by this time acquired both the *do*-transformation and the transposing transformation. What is not clear is whether he went through a prior stage of using non-inverted sentences with *do*. In this connection it is interesting—and possibly revealing—that most of the negative *Why*-questions found 1 1/2 years later, at the beginning of Rune's second stay in Great Britain, were in the majority of cases of the structure predicted in 1967, namely, non-transposed sentences with *do* (in addition to a fair number of more primitive structures):

> Why you don't like and going skiing?
> Why you don't going to school to-yesterday?
> Why Mummy don't play piano now?

It is tempting to speculate that I have accidentally captured an intermediate stage in Rune's development of *Why not-* questions — a productive rule between the last test in March 1966 and the termination of Rune's first stay in Great Britain in June 1966. If so, does it suggest that the process of "forgetting" has been the reverse of learning — a regressive process?

> Why don't you like ice-cream?
> — Why you don't like ice-cream?
> — Why you not like ice-cream?

7.0 *Conclusion*

The purpose of this paper has been to present some of my findings concerning the development of Wh-questions in two Norwegian children acquiring English as a second language and relate them to those of a similar study of first-language acquisition. The presentation has been somewhat biased in that I have chosen to concentrate on the similarities between first- and second-language learners. Taking the age and maturity levels into consideration and the fact that my children already know one language, the similarities are quite striking and not necessarily what one would expect.

The findings have been discussed in the light of the hypotheses put forward by Brown (1968). Brown has been concerned with confirming or disconfirming a development of Wh-questions in children which reflects the transformational derivations in transformational-generative grammar, in order to find out if these might be said to represent psychologically real operations. Brown is cautious in his interpretation of the evidence and recommends that it might be wise to have a second look at empiricist explanations, as they might still throw light on the process of language acquisition.

Although I think nothing conclusive can be said about the psychological reality of the transformational rules discussed in the paper, the transformational description itself has made it possible to set up testable hypotheses. Whether Brown is right or not in his tentative conclusions is of less importance. At the present stage of inquiry into child language development it is of interest to find out what the regularities are across children with regard to the order of emergence of linguistic structures, irrespective of whether or not the development can be predicted from linguistic theory. What we need is a more comprehensive language learning theory, which also takes into account general cognitive factors and not only linguistic mechanisms.

Reprinted from *Occasional Papers,* No. 8 (University of Essex, Language Centre) by permission of the author.

FOOTNOTES

[1] I am indebted to my supervisor, Dr. Terence Moore at the Language Centre, University of Essex, for critical comments and advice on this paper. He is, however, not responsible for the views expressed and my possible misinterpretation of Professor Brown's views, for which I apologize.

[2] See also R. Brown et al. (1969) and Ursula Bellugi (1965).

[3] The team has included also Ursula Bellugi, Colin Fraser, Dan Slobin, Jean Berko Gleason, and David McNeill.

[4]The constituent itself dominates indefinite elements, such as: 'some thing', 'at some place'. For a treatment of questions, see J. J. Katz & P. M. Postal (1964), pp. 79-117.

[5]J. J. Katz & P. M. Postal (1964), pp. 108-112, discuss the distinction between ordinary questions and "echo questions" (Brown's "occasional questions") and propose the introduction of an Emphasis Marker in deep structure to account for this difference.

[6]Nor has it so far been confirmed by the Language Acquisition Research Project at the University of Edinburgh, according to Elisabeth Ingram, "Language development in children" (mimeo).

[7]My research project is supported in full by the Norwegian Research Council for Science and the Humanities.

[8]The equipment used has been a Tandberg stereo tape recorder Model 64x with a footswitch rewind-playback control and a Tandberg tape recorder Model 13, which is a cartridge machine for a one channel repeater system. The two can be connected. Further equipment consists of two Tandberg TM 4 microphones and two headphones AKG, K 50 for stereo and mono respectively. Apart from a few recordings on a portable mono tape recorder, all recordings have been stereo recordings, with a tape speed of 7 1/2 i.p.s. The sound has been of a very high quality.

[9]For a justification of this analysis, see U. Bellugi (1965).

[10]A description in terms of a prefixed NEG or C morpheme followed by a Nucleus is used in Klima & Bellugi (1966) for the early stages, but is not proposed as a hypothesis to account for the word order in sentences of the preposing type.

[11]The same general similarities have been found in the development of negative sentences between my informants and those of Brown and associates. A brief discussion is included in Ravem (1969).

[12]Cf. Katz & Postal (1964), p. 8.

[13]Bellugi (1965), p. 119. See also Klima & Bellugi (1966), pp. 203-4 and "The Growth of Transformations" in McNeill (1966), particularly p. 60.

REFERENCES

Bellugi, Ursula. The development of interrogative structures in children's speech. In K. Riegel (Ed.), *The Development of Language Functions*, Ann Arbor: Michigan Language Development Program, Report No. 8, 1965, 103-137.

Brown, R. The development of wh questions in child speech. *Journal of Verbal Learning and Verbal Behavior*, 7, 1968, 279-290.

Brown, R., Cazden, Courtney and Bellugi-Klima, Ursula. The child's grammar from I to III. In J.P. Hill (Ed.), *Minnesota Symposia on Child Psychology*, Vol. 2. Minneapolis: Univ. of Minn. Press, 1969, 28-73.

Brown, R. and Fraser, C. The acquisition of syntax. In C. N. Cofer and Barbara S. Musgrave (Eds.), *Verbal Behavior and Learning*, New York: McGraw-Hill, 1963, 158-197.

Katz, J. J. and Postal, P. M. *An Integrated Theory of Linguistic Descriptions*, Cambridge, Mass., M.I.T. Press, 1964.

Klima, E. S. and Bellugi, Ursula. Syntactic regularities in the speech of children. In J. Lyons and R. J. Wales (Eds.), *Psycholinguistics Papers,* Edinbrugh University Press, 1966, 37-65.

McNeill, D., Developmental psycholinguistics. In F. Smith and G. A. Miller (Eds.) *The Genesis of Language: A Psycholinguistic Approach.* Cambridge, Mass., M.I.T. Press, 1966, 15-84.

Menyuk, Paula. *Sentences Children Use*, Cambridge, Mass. M.I.T. Press, 1969.

Ravem, R. Language acquisition in a second language environment, *IRAL* 6, 2, 1968, 175-185.

———. First and second language acquisition. Paper given to the BAAL Seminar on Error Analysis, Edinburgh 26-27 April, 1969, (mimeo).